FASTING
— AND —
PRAYER
GOD'S HEALING THERAPIES

HUGH A JENKINS, ND, DC

Copyright © 2022 by Hugh Jenkins

Fasting and Prayer
God's Healing Therapies

All rights reserved.
No part of this work may be used or reproduced, transmitted, stored, or used in any form or by any means graphic, electronic, or mechanical, including but not limited to photocopying, recording, scanning, digitizing, taping, Web distribution, information networks or information storage and retrieval systems, or in any manner whatsoever without prior written permission from the publisher.

An Imprint for GracePoint Publishing (www.GracePointPublishing.com)

GracePoint Matrix, LLC
624 S. Cascade Ave, Suite 201
Colorado Springs, CO 80903
www.GracePointMatrix.com
Email: Admin@GracePointMatrix.com
SAN # 991-6032

A Library of Congress Control Number has been requested and is pending.

ISBN (Paperback): 978-1-951694-73-9
eISBN: 978-1-951694-74-6

Books may be purchased for educational, business, or sales promotional use.
For bulk order requests and price schedule contact:
Orders@GracePointPublishing.com

Dedication

Lord, thank you for your amazing love for me. Thank you for saving those who put their trust in you. Thank you to my wife Gwen, who greatly helped me write this book because she knows the English language much better than I and thank you to my children, grandchildren, great-grandchild, and extended family.

Medical Disclaimer...

This book is for informational purposes only. By providing the information contained herein I am not diagnosing, treating, curing, mitigating, or preventing any type of disease or medical condition. Before beginning any type of natural, integrative, or conventional treatment regimen, it is advisable to seek the advice of a licensed healthcare professional.

Resource Disclaimer...

This book may contain links to other websites or contents belonging to or originating from third parties or links to websites and features in banners or other advertising. Such external links are not investigated, monitored, or checked for accuracy, adequacy, validity, reliability, availability, or completeness by us.

Table of Contents

Table of Contents	v
Why I Wrote this Book	vii
Introduction	xv
List of Terms	xix
Chapter One: History	1
Chapter Two: The Process	9
Chapter Three: Fasting Programs	21
Chapter Four: Fasting Diets	29
Chapter Five: Healthy Foods for Fasting	41
Chapter Six: Healing the Body	57
Chapter Seven: Healing the Mind and Emotions	62
Chapter Eight: Healing the Spirit	69
Chapter Nine: What to Expect When Healing	79
Chapter Ten: Twenty-One-day Devotional	89
More Personal Stories of Fasting	112
About the Author	123
Resources	125

Why I Wrote this Book

"Fasting is nature's operating table"
Dr. Alvenia M. Fulton

"Prayer is God being our inner surgeon"
Dr. Hugh A. Jenkins

When I was in my senior year of high school, a doctor came to do sports physicals for the track team. He said that I had a heart problem, so I had to go to the University of Chicago hospital for a complete cardiac workup. They found that my heart beat irregularly when I was in a passive state like sitting or lying down but when I was on the treadmill running, my heart beat regularly. The doctors asked me if I had ever drank coffee and I said yes. And I had drank coffee, once, during the summer prior to my senior year. That was it. I was released back to training on the track team as a pole vaulter.

    My parents were already into some form of natural living and healing. We took nutritional supplements on a regular basis. After that examination, I read that Vitamin E was great for heart health, so I started taking more than what was in my multiple vitamin and mineral tablets.

My freshman year of college, I had a complete physical, and told the doctor there was something wrong with my heart. After the examination, he told me that my heart was in perfect shape. I have had many exams since that one and my heart continues to be in perfect health. I give credit to the Vitamin E that I still take today.

During my years as an undergrad, I studied pre-med to prepare to go into allopathic medicine. My senior year, I applied to many medical schools, one of them, and my first choice, was the University of Illinois College of Medicine at Chicago, but God had another direction for me.

In 1974, my father introduced me to Dr. Alvenia M. Fulton at a National Health Federation conference in Chicago. He had been a patient of hers four years earlier and fasted under her supervision for twenty-one days without any ill effect. During the meeting with Dr. Fulton, she asked me to come to her office to talk about Naturopathic Medicine and perhaps an opportunity of studying under her. When I met with her, she told me that there are a lot of students going into allopathic medical school, but they needed more students to go to natural medical school.

I learned about the National College of Naturopathic Medicine from her, which is now called National University of Natural Medicine. When I studied their catalog, I found out that their curriculum was identical to the allopathic medical schools, and they had some courses in natural healing that very much interested me. Because of my heart health story, I was personally leaning toward them. I applied and was accepted, and the rest is history.

During school breaks and in the summer, Dr. Fulton allowed me to study the art and science of fasting under her mentorship. She also allowed me to assist her with patients that came from different parts of the world to fast with her. She had tremendous faith in me and allowed me to become part of her staff that traveled to Atlanta, GA in 1975. We supervised 120 people from across the United States on a fast from Christmas Eve of 1975 to New Year's Day of 1976 for world hunger.

She was not only a Naturopathic doctor, but also an ordained Baptist minister, one of the pioneers of natural healing, and one of the world authorities on fasting at that time. Dr. Fulton was a great inspiration from God and a woman of God. She was a self-published author of several natural health books, and it was not surprising to realize that one of the many seeds to write this book was subconsciously planted in my mind many years ago during her mentorship. I praise God for blessing me to know and learn from a great healer like Dr. Fulton.

I have daydreamed about long lines of eager readers waiting for their chance to get a first edition copy of this book during book signings at my former churches (Trinity United Church of Christ on the south side of Chicago and Friendship West Baptist Church in South Dallas) and many other churches throughout the world. Those events continuously remain a vision in my mind.

But I kept putting off getting started on the book. Perhaps there was a delay, I reasoned, because I did not have a burning desire to write this book. Or, when I talked to people about the book, they didn't have a yearning to read about fasting and prayer. It seemed my audience and I were not ready for this venture, yet the desire kept growing in my mind and in my heart. As luck would have it, life came to my rescue. It allowed me to experience various mental, physical, and emotional challenges that clarified the material needed to draw my audience to this important topic.

Looking back at those experiences, I know that I had to go through them to put my story on paper. Many people with whom I have spoken about fasting are now going through or have gone through similar challenges in their lives. Mine took me to a very low point in my life. I was chronically depressed and barely physically functioning and lost my self-esteem.

At one time, I had been a very successful Naturopathic and Chiropractic doctor, but in 2015 my world started to collapse around me. In fact, for quite a few years I did not work at all.

I was so depressed that I avoided eye contact with others because of lack of confidence. In addition to my practice, I also had previously been successful as a natural health and wellness speaker. I lectured locally, nationally, and internationally.

About a year later, my wife told me that I needed to get out of the house and start working again. With so many things happening in my life, I was broken mentally and emotionally, and it negatively impacted my speech. I did not feel it was possible to read a PowerPoint presentation with enthusiasm, so how could I write a book and do live presentations when I was so broken, even if the idea was still floating in my head?

I went to several doctors, therapists, and counselors. Each of them put me through their treatment programs, but I still felt stuck. Something was missing and they did not have the answers. It was at that point I asked one of my counselors if she believed in God and the Holy Spirit. She said yes with a caveat—she could only include a spiritual aspect in the sessions if the client brought it up first. That was the answer to the beginning of my healing journey.

My counselor knew of some of the spiritual leaders, motivational speakers, and other positive people whom I followed. These non-medical leadership ideas became part of my medical intervention and key components of my healing process. Even better, the ideas helped shape a Healing Community that I now lead. "It takes a village to raise a child" is an Igbo and Yoruba proverb that exists in many different African languages. Well, it also takes a village to heal a body, mind, and spirit through fasting as well as prayer. Thank You, God, for our healing!

I understand that the healing journey is an ongoing process, but I have begun to feel whole again. While I have taken baby steps, it has felt like a marathon to get to this point in my journey. There were times when I hit the wall and felt that I could not finish the race. But God is my health and wellness coach. He told me to just take one step and He would take two. "The journey of a thousand miles begins with the first step," noted Lao Tzu and it is true in my experience. The Creator has called on His many guardian angels to be members of my healing community during this very important assignment He has for me.

During my journey, I have had to release past fears to embrace faith in God to reach my healing. I have had to change the little "f" in fear to a big "F" in faith because I realized without faith it is impossible to please God. There are four different aspects to my journey. With the balance of each aspect, my life has been blessed in so many unexpected ways. Through these difficult experiences, I have been touched in each aspect of my mind, body, spirit, and emotions.

I describe in a later chapter my mental fasting when studying for exams as well as my physical fasting effects during my first marathon later in the book. Here are the other two rungs of my ladder to enlightenment through prayer and fasting and why I wrote this book.

Spiritual: Essentially, I wrote this to become closer to God and understand and learn to control my emotions for my mental health.

In 1999, I had a mental and emotional crisis; it seemed to be happening every five years. I finally became conscious that it was a pattern, and in 2014 I reprogrammed myself that it would *not* happen that year, but instead, I'd unconsciously pushed it forward to 2015. That was a mistake. I had a major mental and emotional breakdown. During my healing programs, one of my therapists worked with me spiritually more than physically. This brought me back in balance with God, with the use of fasting and prayers, affirmations, mantras, and meditations. My wife also reminded me that fasting was the roots to my naturopathic medical practice and that I needed to return to my roots, both personally and professionally.

Emotional: During the crisis in 1999 I lost so much weight that I lost faith in fasting because of the fear of being too small. But in my trials of 2015, God showed me that he would not leave me or forsake me and clarified that my healing would only come through fasting and prayers. Being a child of God, I learned that I could fall down but get right back up with faith in Him. This mental emotional journey has proven to be longer and more challenging than the physical one. People can see physical healing, but not emotional healing. It is unseen like faith, but one must have the faith of a mustard seed to endure the trials and tribulations of life's emotional journeys.

For more than forty years I have practiced the healing art of fasting, and I have added prayers to it within the last few decades. I am excited to share the many lessons that I have learned and knowledge that I have acquired involving natural health and wellness with you.

In writing this book, I am first serving God, family, community, and then myself thereby fulfilling my part in the Circle of Life.

Introduction

Have you ever considered how fasting, and praying can uplift your spiritual life, mind, body, and emotions? Have you ever tried doing them on your own without the success that you were searching for? Did you ever think (or were told) to search for someone or something to assist you on your journey? If you are reading this book, then your search has ended.

I have written this book for people who have fasted in the past and are fasting in the present, for those that will fast in the future, as well as people who have never fasted that would love to learn. The goal is how to reach the optimum level of health and wellness.

There are many different types of fast. From the intermittent fast that is done for so many hours a day up to and including the extended fast of forty days. Not everybody can fast for forty days, but everybody can fast.

Fasting has become more popular. Many people regularly do intermittent fasting. Some do it and don't realize it because their first meal is around noon. This is actual the time when most seasoned intermittent fasters have their first meal of the day.

Through the years of assisting thousands of people on their personal fasting journeys, I have learned more from them than they have from me. The most poignant lesson is that by adding prayers to fasting, change occurs, particularly in their health.

Fasting without prayer is incomplete, like playing baseball without a glove or wishing cold hands would be warm without mittens.

God is the master healer, our lead surgeon. He has never lost a patient - each is either healed on earth or in heaven. When God tells you that you need surgery, His surgical procedures are fasting and prayer. If you tell God that you do not either believe in fasting or prayer, it is like telling a surgical doctor that you only want him or her to just cut you open, not remove what is wrong. Your surgery is incomplete and unsuccessful. You are open to more diseases, never to be whole again. That is why God's perfect therapies, fasting and prayers, always work!

In the Bible, it says WHEN you fast and pray not IF you fast and pray. It is a prerequisite and requirement for God's life classes. Taking a leap of faith off a mountaintop either voluntarily or by a push from God, you will land—soft or hard, it is your choice. God gives us all free will.

I have had several people tell me for years, particularly using the Daniel Fast, that they could not fast because their doctors told them they had to eat to take their meds. What is important to note is those same doctors have people fast from four to twelve hours before a fasting blood test, or any routine bloodwork.

Others who have tried but say they would not fast again explain that it is because they love to eat, especially the wrong foods: red meats, sugar, alcohol, or salt, just to name a few toxic foods. I hear all the time, "I'm not going to sacrifice what I love to eat for any fast." The value of fasting is to sacrifice something of a lesser value to acquire something of a much greater value and blessing. It is like holding a penny in a tightly clenched fist instead opening the hand to receive a dollar. People with this attitude have a poverty mindset of their body instead of a prosperous mindset of God's holy temple. As the Bible says, "The spirit is willing, but the flesh is weak."

We need to remember that the blessings of fasting are instructions from God. "Now to Him who is able to do exceedingly abundantly above all that we ask or think, according to the power that works in us," (Ephesians 3:20 NASB1995). People have been studying the physical, mental, spiritual, and emotional benefits of fasting for thousands of years and are still discovering more of God's healing properties daily. Though the spiritual blessing of prayer has been told in many holy books throughout the centuries, not until recently has the scientific community researched and proven that prayer has healing powers.[1]

Adding prayer to fasting is not just fasting and praying—it is fasting times prayer. When you pray and eat, seventy percent of the body's blood is in the digestive system and less is in the brain and other organs which are doing the work of prayer. But when you fast *and* pray, the body sends much more blood to the brain and other organs because it is not needed by the digestive system. When I fasted for four days before and during my first marathon, because seventy percent of the body's blood was not being used by my digestive system, it was used to deliver fuel for my muscles. I set a goal to complete the marathon in four hours; God blessed

---

[1] Andrade and Radhakrishnan, "Prayer and healing."

me with three hours and fifty-eight minutes, and I attribute it to fasting and prayer. I broke my fast with some fruit and a massage.

Fasting takes us further and faster into our God consciousness than prayers can do alone. Fasting fast-tracks our prayers into warp speed. Whatever the desires of your heart for your mind, body, spirit, and emotions, just ask God to bless you with his healing therapies and disciples of fasting and prayer.

Peppered within the book are testimonies of all the people that I have serviced throughout the many decades of my practice. They are examples of how many have received not just a healing but also a blessing. It is important to see that others have done it in the past and have achieved not just positive weight loss, lowering of blood pressure, improved digestion, but also mental clarity, and spiritual awareness. I hope these testimonies will enlighten you on how many have taken the leap of faith and achieved the blessings of God.

List of Terms

Auto-detoxification: detoxification that happens automatically without initiation.

Autolysis: the destruction of cells or tissues by their own enzymes, mainly in dead or dying cells.

Autophagy: the consumption of the body's own cells or tissues in order to remove disease; also, a metabolic process in starvation.

Break-fast: a diet of food or drink that allows the body to recover from a fast.

Cleanse or Cleansing diet: a diet or therapeutic approach that aims to detoxify the body for optimal health.

Diet: a specified schedule of food and drink to aid the body's functions.

Fast: abstaining from food or drink or both for health benefits, ritual acts, religious practices, or ethical reasons.

Herxheimer Reaction: A reaction caused by the use of antimicrobial treatments that break the bacterial cell membranes releasing bacterial toxins into the bloodstream and resulting in a systemic inflammatory response.

Para Cleanse: a type of cleanse most often aimed at the gastrointestinal tract designed to support the health and wellness of the body.

Pre-fast: a diet of food or drink that prepares the body for a fast.

Program of fasting: a diet plan or a set of curated activities that support fasting

Chapter One:
History

Historical and Cultural Fasting

The practice of fasting is a major part of many cultures and has been used for thousands of years. Fasting ranges from restricting certain foods to, in its most extreme form, not eating and drinking for periods of time. The choice of hours, days, and the method of fasting correspond to an individual's health, lifestyle, and goals. The reasons one might fast can depend on the person, family, culture, and community.

Involuntary and Voluntary Fasting

Involuntary fasting is most often linked with a lack of or a shortage of food, commonly referred to as starvation, whereas voluntary fasting is a restriction reflecting a personal or an historical collective choice. Either partial or total fasting may allow the consumption of pure water, which can sometimes be sweetened or combined with organic coffee or herbal tea. There

Fasting and Prayer

are various spiritual, health, religious, and political reasons for fasting.

Fasting Periods in Hinduism

There are several fasting periods in Hinduism. The most popular of them is *Ekadashi*, a monthly fast done during the lunar cycle of each full and new moon, on the eleventh day after each. Humans also go through a forty-to-forty-eight-day cycle called mandala. Refraining from eating because the body does not demand food during these specific days brings an optimum level of vibrant health to the body, mind, spirit, and emotions. It creates the right mindset for us to turn into our inner God.

Another important occasion celebrated at the beginning of each year is to give honor to one of their Gods, Lord Shiva. Shiva represents the motion of life-giving energy in the body.

Shiva is life, the potential for life, the all-encompassing universal soul. Some would call Shiva pure consciousness. It cannot be created nor destroyed, it is like the Alpha and the Omega. During the fasting period, the body is in a state of restful silence to discipline the ego. The meditative mind is in its highest state of awareness, which frees one from thought.

During these two fasting periods there is generally no food or water intake for twenty-four hours from sundown to sundown. These fasts are used as a form of atonement to their god and to thank him for their special blessings.

There is a yearly routine fasting practice in the Hindu religion. The members are not obligated to go through this process, it is a voluntary physical, mental, spiritual, and emotional act of self. The main purpose of this fast is to cleanse and detoxify the body-mind connection to Ganesh, their god of wisdom, success, luck, and the remover of obstacles. There are personal, family, and/or community guidelines that determine the different forms of fasting. Each person determines if their fast is going to be from simple abstaining of one meal or substitution of certain foods. They may also choose a total abstinence of water. In the Hindu tradition, a fasting day of spiritual knowledge can be rewarded with a small part of bliss, *Modaks*, which are sweet dumplings made from coconut and covered with rice or wheat flour.

Various Reasons for Fasting

Jeûne, French for fasting comes from *Jejunare,* the Latin for abstinence and an act of not eating. Fasting is the avoidance of food. Fasting may also mean limiting or not eating or restricting oneself to certain foods. Over the course of history, many populations including the ancient Chinese, Siberians, American Indians, Polynesians, and Celtics have practiced fasting for medical therapies and spiritual reasons.

Ancient Greek athletes' physical training included preparing their bodies during fasting to increase performance prior to the Olympic Games. Taking this example, I prepared for my first marathon by doing a four day fast leading up to the 26.2-mile Chicago Marathon. In addition to scattered historical evidence of physical reasons, it's also considered a way to increase intelligence, clear insight, and to promote mental clarity.

Using this as a successful illustration of excellence, during my attendance in both naturopathic and chiropractic medical schools, I fasted from one to three days prior to quizzes, midterms, finals, and board exams to increase my mental clarity with great success.

The major religions also imposed annual fasts centuries later, Lent for Catholics and Ramadan for Muslims, during which time the fasters deprive themselves of certain foods. Over the centuries, these fasts evolved into Catholics having meatless Fridays and Muslims not eating from sunup to sundown during Ramadan.

It is widely believed that the Hunzas of the North India Himalayas fast to prepare for a new phase of spiritual existence.

Inedia, another Latin name for fasting, also called air or dry fasting. Because nothing is consumed either of food or water. It is the ability to live without these substances. Sustaining the body only on air, sunlight, or the universal energy, known as Qi. It was valued by the church in the Middle Ages as a spiritual fasting practice. It has been rumored that some East Indian holy people and Tibetan Buddhists practice this and may still be practicing it.

Lent, for centuries, has been a particularly strict period of the year from Ash Wednesday to Easter Sunday. For many, it involves sexual abstinence, elimination of meats as well as sometimes eggs and dairy products. Originally, it was a time for prayer, forgiveness, and repentance. The practice of Lent is less integrated in society today, but fasting has remained, both for religious and secular reasons.

Lenten Obligations

Lent is the strictest fast observed by the Christian Church. It begins on Ash Wednesday and lasts forty days. It is a time of prayer, repentance, and cleansing in preparation for the Easter celebrations.

Fasting in the Present Day

Nowadays, fasting during Lent is no longer as much of an obligation. Those who wish to fast during this period may choose to give up certain pleasures, such as sweets or alcohol that have been proven to be harmful to one's health. Outside of the many religious practices, fasting is practiced for health and wellness. Detox therapies may replace standard daily food with fruit and vegetable juices, while some clinics offer total fasting programs.

Every religion has this common thread of fasting. Many of them are practiced at the same or different times of the year. But they all are done with a preparation before, during, and afterwards to get maximum physical and spiritual enlightenment.

Testimonials

Bahati Merchant

My name is Bahati Merchant and I have known Dr. Hugh Anthony Jenkins since the day his family moved into the neighborhood. As youngsters, we were inseparable. The kind of yin and yang that makes a friendship have depth and longevity. From an early age, both of our parents taught us the need to strive for excellence. Not just our parents, but the whole community supported our journey interested in science. We won first place at a coveted sixteenth district high school science fair. Way back then Tony and I made a pact, it said we would grow, study, and learn many things. Mostly how to heal ourselves and others. Holistic medicine was new and not readily accepted. We agreed to go our separate ways both towards what we believed enlightenment was. But most important to come back together and share life lessons.

So, it is with great honor to be asked to participate in such an important healing doctrine. Dr. Jenkins' main goal is to heal through science and God's wisdom.

I do not know very much about other healing ways, I only immersed myself in one. That being from Java Indonesia where I have spent the last thirty-five years of my life back and forth from my home here on the big island of Hawaii.

Java, like Hawaii, shimmers in the middle of the sea, surrounded by the spirituality of oceans and volcanoes. Early Javanese culture sought to make a connection between man and the Creator. This theory is inseparable from the ancient civilization of java culture.

Central Javanese believed everything man needed to thrive was here in one form or another. These ways of wisdom guided their everyday lives. Martial arts and medicine were all connected by a thin thread. This thread could be utilized during the process of fasting.

To be clear, fasting was more than a restriction of food to the ancient Javanese. Fasting was a prerequisite for meditation and all healing exercises of "Labuhan" had their interplay.

In the central Javanese spiritual Healing Art of Sagen. Through the Javanese fasting it also means abstinence of many things, during a preset time. One seeks to connect to the universe by abstaining from drugs, coffee, sugar, sex, and even, for periods of time, sleep. By giving up these worldly things your body utilizes in the very finest of ways every particle of your being.

Prayers are recited at intervals that correspond with the type of fast. Fasting for health requires knowledge of healing. Fasting to enhance one's spirituality and prayers are uniquely different. In my personal experience one must do specific measures to ensure specific desired results.

Meditation takes on a new meaning from the Javanese spiritual art of Sajen. Finger locking positions commonly known as Mudras are incorporated with specific breathing rhythms that are designed to bring the practitioner closer to the true meaning of life.

Movements during "Meditasi" help to invigorate the mind, body, and soul.

Grounding in your energy while sliding your feet across the sand gives you a feeling of indescribable joy. All this is brought into play and heightened by purposely fasting. In my teacher's words, to cleanse oneself through the art of fasting we open the door of all possibilities.

Many fasts that I have done require no water, no eating and not even sleeping for forty-eight to seventy-two hours. This can be difficult without the help of a guru or a teacher. I have been blessed to have them all.

It is through Lakutam Pusaka Sakti Mataram that this information emanates in the heart of the jungle, where nature and energy come together. Fasting becomes more than just not eating, it becomes an integral inseparable function.

Thanks, Dr. Jenkins, for this opportunity. I know Garfield and Phyllis are smiling from above on you.

Chapter Two:
The Process

Fasting

It is not so simple to just jump in and out of a fasting program. The length of the pre-fast preparation depends on the type and length of the fast. The preparation is much different for a short intermittent fast compared to a forty-day water fast or a dry fast.

The Pre-Fast

Though the trendy term now is a *cleansing diet*, the original nomenclature has historical value. In my training with my mentor, Dr. Fulton, she would assign her patients a five-day cleansing diet of herbal tea, protein drinks, and pure fruit juices, advising them to eat only fresh fruits and refrain from bananas. No other foods would be eaten during the five days. Though healthy, this five-day cleansing diet would not totally cleanse the body because it takes a minimum of ninety days to cleanse down to the cellular level. After the five days, Dr. Fulton then put her patients on a twenty-one-day supervised fast of only distilled water, lemon juice, and honey even if they had never fasted a day in their life.

In my many years of practice, I have personally limited myself to her five-day cleansing diet during the pre-fast. The health of the average American has declined, with that impairment beginning at a younger age than ever before. Our children are having diseases such as high blood pressure, diabetes, and arthritis, that just a hundred years ago were only seen in the older population. As a result, I have modified and extended the cleansing program for up to ninety days depending on the health needs of the patient.

After I evaluate my clients, I combine cleansing herbs specifically for the causes of the imbalances in their bodies rather than for the diseases they have been diagnosed with. I use up to twenty different medicinal herbs. The juices suggested are diluted fifty-fifty with distilled, alkaline, or probiotic water. The foods they eat are not just fruits, which can be exceptionally high in sugars, therefore other raw plant foods are also included. The reason for that is because of the increase in diabetes and pre-diabetes, just to name one of the many preventable diseases caused by an unhealthy diet.

The length of the pre-fast is related to the type and length of the fast. It can range from one day to one month. During my Fasting and Prayer Community's monthly seven-day wellness challenges, the pre-fast is the first three days leading into the fast, which is the maximum of twenty-four hours.

The pre-fast starts a diet to eliminate certain foods and ingredients from the diet for optimal cleansing: processed sugars, salts, processed food, animal products, yeast, refined white grains, deep-fried food, solid fats, chocolate, coffee or caffeinated drinks, and alcohol. As the days progress, more foods are eliminated until the intake is limited to totally raw plant foods. This process allows the body to transition smoothly into fasting.

The Tiao He Cleanse and Para-Cleanse Program

I have studied Acupuncture and Traditional Chinese Medicine (TCM) in China and the US. Using the best of both worlds, I have used a Chinese-Western blend of herbs for cleansing also as a pre-fast program for many years.

The Tiao He Cleanse, and the Para-Cleanse program use both the eastern and western methods and are often paired together for maximum efficacy. These programs have shown to be very successful for my clients throughout the years. The period of cleansing is a minimum of twenty to twenty-five days, of which the Tiao He Cleanse is ten to fifteen, and the Para-Cleanse is just ten days. A person who feels they need more cleansing and may possibly have parasites such as Candida, can do the Para-Cleanse for ten days on and off for a period suitable to them and their personal needs.

Tiao He Cleanse

In Chinese, *Tiao He* means reconcile or cause to coexist in harmony and can be used to:

- Support the entire intestinal system.
- Support intestinal metabolism and regulation.
- Improve energy, harmony, and a sense of well-being.

It is an ideal program for beginners and others who want to start their first or successive herbal programs. This is a great cleanser for any season like spring cleansing and ideal as a pre-fasting program or to prepare for a weight loss-management program.

A fifteen-day nutritional herbal program is designed to help the body achieve optimum levels of balance and harmony. It combines Chinese and Western nutritional herbal knowledge and experience and is designed to support the cleansing mechanisms of the body by targeting the intestinal, digestive, and circulatory systems.

This program consists of :

- Chinese Liver Balance TCM Concentrate, an herbal blend that protects and supports healthy liver, gallbladder, spleen, and stomach function.

- All Cell Detox, an herbal blend that detoxifies the body and strengthens the eliminative organs' function: colon, kidneys, and liver. Improve digestion and absorption of nutrients to help nutritional deficiencies in the body.

- Lower Bowel Stimulator, an herbal blend that stimulates the production of bile and other digestive fluids to promote colon peristaltic action for healthy elimination, enhance function of the liver, balance the pH, and eliminate intestinal parasites and worms.

- Psyllium hulls are a great dietary source of fiber which are effective in restoring and/or maintaining regular easy healthy bowel movements.

- Burdock root, a tonic and alternative herb, also known as a "blood purifier", increases vitality by improving the breakdown and excretion of toxins and waste.

- Black walnut has historically been used to expel intestinal worms, mild laxative functions, and enhances the liver's detoxifying functions.

Para Cleanse

A ten-day nutritional herbal program that supports and cleanses the digestive system, emphasizes eliminating parasites but it also improves liver function and supports immune function.

- Supports intestinal system function.
- May help improve bowel function.
- Cleanses and detoxifies.

Many people experience undesirable gastrointestinal effects as a result of activities that include traveling internationally, eating undercooked foods, drinking contaminated water, exposure to daycare centers, having a pet or even the prescribed use of antibiotic drugs. Fortunately, the herbal formulas included in Para-Cleanse may help improve bowel function and support the body's cleansing and detoxification process while also helping make the intestines inhospitable to foreign invaders.

This program consists of:

- Herbal Pumpkin is an herbal blend that rids the body of parasites in the digestive system and improves bowel function.
- Black Walnut ATC Concentrate has historically been used to expel intestinal worms, it encourages mild laxative functions, and enhances the liver's detoxifying functions.
- Artemisia Combination is an herbal blend that helps to eliminate parasites, soothe inflamed tissues, improve digestion, and bowel elimination.
- Paw Paw Cell-Reg supports the immune system function

The Master Cleanse

The Master Cleanse is perhaps one of the simplest and safest ways to cleanse, detox, and lose weight. The original version, otherwise known as the lemonade diet, has been around close to fifty years. It's one of the easiest, most delicious, and effective cleansing and weight loss diets available. You can feel good and get rid of what ails you. This diet has been used for every health problem with great success.[2]

The basic causes of disease are the unhealthy habits of a toxic diet, lack of exercise, negative mindset, lack of spiritualism, and negative emotions, which makes fasting and cleansing very relevant in today's sedentary society.

People build strong, healthy bodies from a healthy diet and positive lifestyle or they create diseased bodies from a toxic unhealthy diet and negative lifestyle.

Lemons are one of the richest food sources of vitamins and minerals. Being a citrus fruit, they are acidic outside of the body but alkalizing inside. Disease cannot exist in an alkaline environment but cleansing and detoxification is accentuated in one.

THE MASTER CLEANSE OR LEMONADE DIET

This diet is a ten-day program, although some have used this diet for up to forty days. It can be used seasonally, three to four times a year. As the external environment changes so will your

---

[2] Burroughs, *Master Cleanser*.

internal environment. Regularly doing this program does wonders for keeping the body in an optimum state of health and wellness.

- Cleanse and eliminate toxins in all the body's systems.
- Purifies down to the cellular level and for assimilation of nutrients to build healthy tissues and organs.
- Eliminates weight/waste during a weight management program for one who is overweight or obese.
- Promotes digestive health when the system needs to rest and rejuvenate during fasting and prayer programs.

This is one of the easiest cleansing diets to try. Below I am including the recipe so that you can try it when you are ready. As I've mentioned before, if you have not fasted before, please start slow and simple with professional assistance if it is available.

Several of my clients have used the Master Cleanse, and some have used it repeatedly.

THE MASTER CLEANSE RECIPE

2 Tablespoons organic lemon juice
2 Tablespoons organic maple syrup
1/10 Teaspoon organic cayenne pepper
8 oz purified, distilled, or alkaline water

Combine the juice, maple syrup, and cayenne pepper with the water.

Shake it up and drink.

The Break-fast

The most important part of any fasting program is the break fast. You can go into a fast wrong and you can also fast wrong, but if you break the fast wrong, you can literally shock your body. It has been recorded that some people have aggravated their previous health problems after breaking the fast incorrectly.

Your body lets you know when it is time to break the fast. One indicator is your tongue. During a fast, if your tongue has a thick white coating it is an indication that your body is toxic. When the coating of your tongue is clear and pink, it is the time to break the fast.

Another indicator is your appetite. About day three or four you lose the urge to eat and there is no hunger. When the hunger returns, your body has consumed all the surplus energy stored that is not needed for basic function. If you do not break the fast, your body will go from a fasting mode into a starvation mode.

Other symptoms that could indicate it is time for the fast to end are feeling very weak and fatigued with lightheadedness and dizziness, but may also include brain fog, disorientation, insomnia, and other sleep disturbances. You can have one or all these indicators that tell your body it is time to break your fast. Do not ignore the innate intelligence of your body and attempt to continue to go without food—you can do more harm than good. It is very important to listen to and obey your God consciousness.

Just like the pre-fast, there is a time factor to breaking the fast. The breaking period is one day of breaking for every five days of fasting, or even after three days. With a water-only fast from seven to forty days, take a one day of break-fast for every two days of abstaining from food. It takes time to wake up the digestive system that has been dormant during this time.

If you have been fasting for twenty-one or more days, you cannot just jump back into the Standard American Diet (SAD) of heavy meats, potatoes, processed foods, junk foods, and other unhealthy dead food to wake your digestive system. The longer you fast, the deeper the sleep of your digestive system and the longer it will take to wake it up. Therefore, the formula to break the fast is one day of breaking for every three to five days of fasting. For example, to break a twenty-one-day water fast, your breaking period is four to five days, depending on the health of your digestive and other bodily systems prior to your fast.

Initially, the best thing to break a long water fast is freshly squeezed fruit or vegetable juice diluted fifty-fifty with alkaline or probiotic water. Drink between sixteen to thirty-two ounces of this mixture. After this initial dose, consume eight to sixteen ounces of room temperature to warm vegetable or bone broth. If your digestive system was less than optimum before your fast, add between one to four ounces of Aloe Vera gel to the broth. This mixture will help to coat, heal, and strengthen your digestive system.

Aloe Vera gel is more beneficial for the digestive system than juice because the juice will just go straight through, whereas the gel will coat and heal it faster. For instance, if there is a problem with leaky gut syndrome, the combination of gel and broth can help close the leaks. It is important to continue with this vegetable or bone broth and Aloe Vera gel mixture for the duration of the breaking period.

On the third day of your break-fast, you can introduce small amounts of raw and slightly steamed vegetables. The best vegetables should be prebiotic vegetables such as dandelion greens, Jerusalem artichoke, garlic, onions, asparagus, burdock root, flaxseeds, jicama root, and seaweed. These prebiotics and others are high in dietary fibers that increase the friendly colon bacteria, which helps to strengthen and support the digestive system's health and boost the immune system. Prebiotics have been known to prevent certain chronic preventable diseases and improve metabolic health and wellness.

On the last day of your break-fast you can eat other fruits and vegetables as well as add whole grains, or gluten-free grains if you have a gluten intolerance. The more colorful your foods, the higher energy and healthier your body will become. Certain colors such as red, orange, yellow, green, blue, indigo, and white, just to name a few, have the healthy vibrational energy to balance your organs and chakras.

After your breaking period, your eating lifestyle should be a plant-based diet of fifty-one to seventy-five percent of fruits, vegetables, whole grains, and small amounts of meats. During your fast, your body will reduce to a healthier weight. Your internal organs will have also reduced in size. For example, your stomach should be the size of your fist but for many it has been stretched out by chronically overeating, eating too often, and too late in the day.

After a fast, your body is more sensitive to the toxic foods from the Standard American Diet (SAD) of processed meats, alcohol of any kind, soft drinks, gluten, and junk foods. A healthier diet will continue the benefits of the fast to optimize the body to health and wellness.

Doing a healthy break-fast enables the body to go back into fasting in the future with little or no challenges as in previous fasts. Your body is cleaner, healthier, stronger, and biologically younger.

Prayer

For greater success with fasting, prayer is encouraged.

In the past, there were a variety of ways people prayed. Some people would go into their prayer closet, get down on their knees, and prepare to commune with God. At the end of their prayer session, they would say Amen, thank God for his grace and mercy, rise from their knees, leave their prayer closet, and would try to sin no more.

Others would lie face down on their hands and knees in groups and pray up to five times a day. Another style would use their prayer or meditation altars in their homes to pray and/or chant, light incense, use prayer beads, crystals, etc. Many different cultures and religions would repeat refrains before, during, and after their prayer sessions. The same dedication to ritual is very important, perhaps more so when doing a fasting program.

Choose the type of prayer you will rely on and be just as consistent as your fast.

Testimonials
Glenn Moore

My favorite fasting and cleansing is the master cleanser. I like it because it changed my life in many ways. When I first started, I was pushing 190 lbs., but I took off more than 20 lbs. in almost two weeks. I would have to give myself about a week or two before I started to get my mind set on doing it. I would go over the book from front to back to prepare myself. The first three days were the hardest to get my body adjusted to the cleanse. It lasted for ten days then I would have a three-day coming off period. The night before I started, I would drink a cup of Smooth Move tea to prepare for my first elimination in the morning. I would drink thirty-two oz. of warm sea salt water, wait forty-five minutes to an hour, and be prepared to go to the washroom for my elimination. Then I would start drinking some of my lemonade tea that I made in advance. I usually make a gallon or two to put in the refrigerator. It's a mixture of fresh lemon juice, organic maple syrup, thirty-two oz. of water, and cayenne pepper. I would do that for ten days with three-days coming off. I've been doing it for over twenty-five years for three or four times a year. It keeps my weight in tack and my energy levels up, I feel like a new person once I finish it. Once I finish, I go about my regular activities and work out at the gym.

Chapter Three: Fasting Programs

Different Lengths and Times of Fasting

There are many different lengths and times of intermittent fasting. They vary in the number of hours and days of the intermittent fasting, which involves abstinence from food for a set amount of time before eating again. Scientific research suggests that intermittent fasting offers benefits such as fat loss, better weight management, more vibrant health, and increased longevity. Fasting endorsers claim that an intermittent fasting program is easier to maintain because it has become part of their lifestyle than traditional, weight loss diets, which are temporary. Each individual person's experience of intermittent fasting is unique, and the different lengths and times should be a vibrational match for each person.

There are many ways of intermittent fasting, and people prefer different styles. Here are more details about different ways to experience and enjoy intermittent fasting.

Twelve hours (half-a-day fast)

This is perhaps the simplest form of fasting. A person decides on what half of the day to do the twelve-hour fasting period. Research shows that fasting for ten to sixteen hours, with twelve hours being in the midrange, can cause the body to go into ketosis and burn fat for fuel. This burning encourages weight loss if followed by a healthy plant-base diet.

This simple intermittent fasting program may be a good start for beginners considering adding fasting to their current lifestyle. This fasting window is relatively short, with much of it occurring naturally during sleep. The easiest way to do this twelve-hour fast is to include the period of two hours before sleep, eight hours of sleep and two hours after waking up, the time before the break fast.

As an example, a person could choose to eat their last meal no later than 8 p.m. In bed, asleep no later than 10 p.m., wake up at 6 a.m. and break their fast at 8 am.

Sixteen hours (intermittent fast)

A sixteen-hour fasting day with eight hours of an eating window is called the 16:8 method. This is the most popular intermittent fast. This type of fast may be the next most helpful step for those who have tried the twelve-hour fast without the overnight results they expected.

In this fast, people usually finish their dinner no later than 8 p.m. with their break-fast at noon the next day.

Fasting one to two days weekly

People following this 6:1 or 5:2 fasting, eat the standard amounts of healthy plant-based foods for five to six days and reduce calorie intake on the other one to two days. During the fasting days, men's ideal food intake is about six hundred high nutrient calories and women intake is about five hundred high nutrient calories. Anything under four hundred calories is not fasting, it's starvation.

These fasting days are usually separated in the week. Example, if someone fasts on Monday and Thursday, he or she should eat a healthy plant-based diet on the other days. There should be at least one to two eating days between fasting days.

A limited research study found on this 6:1 or 5:2 diet, which is known as the Fast diet, involved 107 overweight or obese women who found significant weight loss. It also resulted in reduced insulin levels and improved insulin sensitivity among participants with Type II Diabetes.

Alternate day fasting

There are different variations of the alternate day fasting plan that involves fasting every other day or every two days. Alternate day fasting means a complete abstinence of solid foods on those fasting days, while others are eating up to 500 calories. On days of eating, people often eat as much as they want to.

This alternate day fasting is an extreme form of intermittent fasting, especially when attempted by a beginner or those people with certain medical conditions. It may also be difficult to maintain this type of fasting as part of one's lifestyle.

Twenty-four to thirty-six-hour weekly fast

This is my favorite fast. I have used this practice for forty years to maintain my own personal health. A complete fasting period of one day a week for twenty-four to thirty-six hours involves eating no food for that period. People who fast for twenty-four hours do it from breakfast to breakfast, lunch to lunch or dinner to dinner. People who fast for thirty-six hours do it from breakfast of one day to lunch on the next day, lunch the first day to dinner the next day, or dinner one day to breakfast on the third consecutive day. I have fasted one day per week for many years, between twenty-four to thirty-six hours. I extend that one day per week to three days per month by adding on an additional forty-eight hours.

On this fasting program, people can drink distilled, spring, or alkaline water, herbal teas, fresh fruit and veggie juices, bone broth, smoothies, and other nutrient-dense drinks during their fasting period.

When people return to eating, they should consume a healthy plant-based diet. Eating in this manner reduces a person's total empty calorie intake but does not limit the specific healthy foods that they eat.

A twenty-four to a thirty-six hour fast may be challenging at the beginning and it may cause some minor problems. Some side effects, such as fatigue caused by not drinking enough fluid, especially water, headaches caused by toxicity and dehydration, or irritability from either being hungry or having low blood sugar. People found that over time, the body adjusts to this new lifestyle of fasting and these challenges become less and less prominent.

Three-days per month fasting

The three days a month fast is just an extension of the one day fast yet increasing the number of hours to a total of seventy-two. Besides the body getting used to fasting, the spirit also goes through the power of prayer.

During this three-day fasting period, I and others have experienced a lot of positive physical, mental, spiritual, and emotional changes that started and continued even after this short fast is over. There may be changes such as weight loss of an average of a pound or so a day. Bowel and body detoxification happens because it continues detoxification during this and beyond. Reduction of inflammation continues because the liquid that they're drinking have anti-inflammatory properties. Loss of craving of addictive substance, specifically food cravings, also happen. Tumors and other toxic growth may be eliminated because the body goes through a process of Autophagy (auto toxicity).

Seven, fourteen, or twenty-one days fasting every season

The seven-day fast is just an extension of the three-day fast. The first three to four days are challenging for some people because they are having hunger pangs and feel that they must eat. By adding the prayer component, they will find that faith strengthens, and their faith to continue fasting builds.

Like the shorter fast, people can drink the same fluids during a seven-day fast. These same fluids are also allowed during other longer fasts.

The seven to twenty-one-day fasting and prayer programs are excellent to do seasonally because as your external environment changes, so will your internal environment. Historically, many people and cultures have fasted during their yearly external Spring Cleaning so both environments are in sync.

If you have any health issues, especially chronic ones such as high blood pressure, diabetes, arthritis, overweight or obesity, you should be monitored by a qualified healthcare professional who has knowledge and experience in fasting.

Forty-days water fasting (twice yearly)

A forty-day water fast is one of the most extensive, thorough fasts, and it definitely requires medical supervision. It is not advisable to do a forty-day fast if you have not undertaken several shorter ones. Daily, each person is given a gallon of distilled water to drink. If you consume that gallon before the day was finished, you could get another one.

Depending on how long you have had chronic health issues, your body will experience several changes during these forty days. One changes your body may experience is called the "Healing Crisis," which can be physical and spiritual.

My wife went on a forty day fast and corrected the female issues she had for many years. You can read her story in the testimony chapter.

Air fast (now called dry fast)

People have asked me for many years about going on the air/dry fast. I will advise against if they have any health issues related to dehydration. By already being in a state of dehydration the fast would aggravate their health conditions.

During the seven-day water fast from Christmas Eve of 1975 to New Year's Day of 1976 in Atlanta, GA, I did a three-day air fast. Dr. Fulton told me that I was doing it at the right time, in the middle of a water fast. Going into and out of the air fast on a water fast was the best way for me.

The first day of this air fast was a challenge because my energy levels hit rock bottom. Dr. Fulton told me to make sure to take a shower and an enema daily to get the water into my body through my skin and colon. She also told me to tap into the energy of our daily prayers and meditations. By doing those two things, I super-hydrated and super energized to the point that my energy levels soared sky high. It was very important I had my energy because I had to assist Dr. Fulton with the 120 people who were fasting.

Whatever fasting and prayer program you choose, watch how God will bless your mind, body, spirit, and emotions.

How to Choose Your Type of Fast

Out of the many different types of fasts, you can choose the one that best resonates with you from the Daniel Diet, the many different types of intermittent fasts, one day per week, three day per month, seven to fourteen days per season and the forty day fast. As we age, our bodies can't handle long fast that we use to do in our youth. I can personally testify about that with my long history of fasting.

Fasting may seem to be demanding and intense physically, emotionally, and spiritually but when combined with prayer, the results are positive and fantastic. This is when you get the most benefits of your life from God.

People Who Should Not Fast

Even though everybody fasts when they are sleeping, there are a few who should not go beyond that even with proper supervision by a health practitioner who is knowledgeable and experienced is fasting. Pregnant diabetic women, nursing mothers, people who are severely anemic or in a state of starvation (cachexia). And those who have no faith in God's healing therapies of fasting and prayer.

Testimonials

Magdalene Moore

My favorite method for fasting is intermittent fasting. Whenever I use this method, I see results very quickly. It is a pattern I plan to put into full effect in the new year. I eat dinner between 6 and 8 p.m. latest, and I take nothing but my Chinese herbal teas. It works best if I go to bed by 11 p.m. so I don't begin to feel hungry or have cravings. I tend to awaken by 6:30 a.m., so at that point I have more herbal teas and water then prepare for my day. I tend to eat a fruit and a breakfast food that is not sugary by 9:00 a.m. Some days I wait until 12:00 p.m. to eat. I then eat lunch four hours later of protein and vegetable. I tend not to eat poultry nor soy products for protein, and dairy. Since I cannot do an abundance of raw unless they are juiced, which I would have once a week. Dinner is my lightest meal of the day and would be a stir fry of vegetables in avocado oil and a carb. I believe in blessing my food before putting it in my mouth and thanking God for its bounty and its contribution to my good health. During a focused period of fasting, I do not eat anything that walks, flies, or swims nor their offspring, it's vegan time. If I do this for two weeks straight the positive results are obvious.

Chapter Four:
Fasting Diets

What is Commonly Consumed During a Fast

Because of the many different types and lengths of fast, people will eat and drink different foods and liquids. During a food restriction diet or a fast such as the Daniel Fast, people eat fruits, veggies, and other meatless meals. On a Mono diet, only one type of food is consumed.

Daniel Fast

The Daniel Fast is based on the Book of Daniel, from chapter, "Please test your servants for ten days and let us be given some vegetables to eat and water to drink (verse 12)" and Daniel 10:2-3, "In those days, I, Daniel, had been mourning for three entire weeks. I did not eat any tasty food, nor did meat or wine enter my mouth." Many churches implement this fasting diet at the beginning of the year by either starting the first or second week of January. It emphasizes a plant-based diet and pure water. It prohibits the consumption of all flesh and their byproducts, refined processed foods, alcohol, coffee, and other caffeinated beverages.

When I think of the Daniel Fast, I see it as more of an elimination diet than a fast because in my fasting training, Dr. Fulton taught that fasting is the absence of all solid food. While I've encouraged many people to follow the Daniel Fast, and evidence has revealed that this complete twenty-one-day elimination diet leaves clients feeling much better. However, a return to the Standard American diet of toxicity can leave the person feeling that it was bad for them.

The Daniel Fast Diet

From Dr. Fulton's teaching, true fasting is the absence of solid foods. This twenty-one-day /diet plan is different from intermittent fasting because it does not restrict the time that you eat, it restricts *what* you eat. It is more a spiritual connection with God and generally a whole food, plant-based, and vegetarian-vegan diet.

Here is the general Daniel Diet menu:

- **Fruits:** mainly fresh or frozen, not canned and ideally low-glycemic fruits; berries, apples, peaches, grapefruits, cherries, and grapes. This is not an exhausted list.

- **Vegetables:** fresh or frozen, not canned and ideally low-glycemic vegetables; carrots, cucumbers, kale, onions, spinach, and tomatoes. Sweet potatoes are great low-glycemic vegetables and can be eaten in abundance. This is not an exhaustive list.

- **Whole Grains:** whole, unrefined, gluten free, and ideally low-glycemic grains; barley, bulgur wheat, brown rice, steel-cut oats, quinoa, and oat bran. Breads made without yeast; unleavened, whole grain and flatbreads. This is not an exhausted list.

- **Legumes:** dried, unsalted canned varieties and ideally low-glycemic legumes; black beans, chickpeas, lentils, and other bean varieties. This is not an exhausted list.

- **Nuts & Seeds:** mainly raw, unsalted dry-roasted and ideally low-glycemic nuts; walnuts, macadamias, hazelnuts, almonds, cashews, and seeds; pumpkin, sunflower, chia, or flax. This is not an exhausted list.

- **Essential Fatty Acids (EFAs), Oils:** fresh, cold pressed, extra virgin and ideally low-glycemic; Avocado, coconut, grapeseed, olive, sesame, and walnut oils are all healthy options.

- **Herbs & Spices:** mainly organic onion, garlic, ginger, cayenne, cinnamon, turmeric, and a host of many other fresh medicinal herbs and spices will be key in flavoring meals. This is not an exhausted list.

My personal experience of doing the Daniels diet for many years with my church, I have only eaten fruits, vegetables, whole grains, nuts, and seeds. Raw or slight cooked in cold pressed oils and seasoned with organic medicinal herbs. Because there is a wide variety of these foods, I have advised people to eat the ones of their liking.

The Mono Diet

The mono-diet is one of the most effective ways to support and boost the body's natural detoxification. It refers to eating just one type of food (grapes or watermelon as an example) for a designated time, for a minimum of three to five days. However, on other healthy detoxification diets, we should eat a wide variety of seasonal organic fruits, vegetables, nuts, grains, and legumes that are all nutrient dense.

When we are eating just one type of food, the body needs to produce fewer digestive enzymes than when we are eating a combination of foods. When it is producing and utilizing fewer enzymes, the body has plenty of extra energy to redirect its other natural cleansing processes. The mono diet frees up extra energy from digestion for detoxification to the cellular level for cellular repair, and regeneration.

The traditional Ayurvedic diet for detox and recovery is a mono-diet, which can be used anytime when your body is run down, diseased, and needs to be repaired and rejuvenated.

The Grape Diet

The grape diet is one of the oldest and most popular of the mono diets since grapes have a long abundant history. They have grown wild since prehistoric times and have been cultivated in Asia since 5000 BC. There are numerous bible stories and hieroglyphics in ancient Egyptian burial tombs referring to the grape as the "Fruit of the Vine."

Johanna Brandt the author of the *Grape Cure* shares her personal story of living with cancer and her discovery of the healthy properties of grapes. She claims they cured her disease by purifying and rebuilding her body at the cellular level using the science of Naturopathic Medicine, a science she describes as fascinating, and her readers are encouraged to detoxify their bodies and prevent disease through a combination of fasting, prayer, and a diet of organic, seeded grapes.

Grapes contain several important nutrients and powerful plant compounds that benefit health. Having sugar, they do not appear to raise the blood sugar level because of their low glycemic index. The antioxidants in grapes, such as resveratrol, reduce inflammation and may help protect the body against cancer, heart disease, and diabetes. Grapes are easy to incorporate into your diet, whether fresh, frozen, or as juice. For the healthiest benefits, choose fresh organic, seeded red grapes over white grapes.[3]

Some Health Benefits of The Grape Diet

Integrating grapes into your diet helps to increase and maintain the optimum health of the cardiovascular, immune, skeletal, digestive, reproductive, brain, and nervous systems.

- Grapes are beneficial for promoting the health of eyes, colon, heart, lungs, stomach, skin, hair, and balancing the blood sugar. They are beneficial in maintaining a healthy weight during and after weight loss and protecting the brain against mental dysfunction and decline.

- They are high in antioxidants, anti-inflammatory, anti-aging, antimicrobial, and antiviral properties. Nutritional components include folic acid, lutein, calcium, copper, magnesium, manganese, riboflavin, thiamine, vitamin A (as beta-carotene), B6, C, D, E, K, nitrates, iron, potassium, soluble and insoluble fiber.

- They are high in melatonin for better sleep.

- Grapes are loaded with over 1,600 bioactive compounds. The dark red and purple grapes contain more antioxidants

---

[3] Groves, "Health Benefits of Eating Grapes."

than white or green types and are great for the root and crown chakras.

Watermelon Diet[45]

An apple a day keeps the doctor away. But did you know that the watermelon also fits into that category. Being that it is so healthy, and over 90 percent water, makes it one of the best fruits for people having any health issues related to dehydration. Such as high blood pressure, obesity, constipation, other digestive problems, and diabetes. Many people feel that they are hungry, especially during the first few days of fasting. that is more a state of thirst from dehydration than from hunger of food.

It is a fantastic fruit proven to curb a sweet tooth of diabetics., prediabetics, and others because of its natural sugar content of about six percent. Its fiber content as a carbohydrate is over one gram. That with the high percent of water gives you a feeling of fullness. It contains vitamin C, vitamin A (as beta carotene), potassium, and lycopene. The seeded watermelons are healthier because the seeds contain more fiber than seedless watermelons. Your body will function at a higher optimum level, meaning that it will be well hydrated on a watermelon mono diet or other times when eating it.

Research conducted at the University of Kentucky showed that eating watermelon improves lipid profiles and lowers fat accumulation. Because of all the health benefits of watermelon, it

---

[4]https://www.sciencedaily.com/releases/2011/10/111027125153.htm#citation_mla

is not an official diet; it is more like a cleansing program. Boosting weight loss and ridding the body of excess water, toxins, waste, salt, and other impurities. There is no harm in following this program for three to seven days if you're generally in good health. It will help jumpstart your weight loss efforts, then continue it with a liquid fasting program or a healthy plant-based diet.

Red and Yellow Watermelon[6]

Red watermelons, like tomatoes, get their red color from the phytonutrient lycopene. Lycopene is very beneficial for the heart, prostate health, and certain types of cancer. Possible gastrointestinal distress can be caused by consumption of an excess of red watermelons because of its cleansing and detoxification properties.

Yellow watermelons get their yellow color from their richness in beta-carotene, They're high in magnesium, iron, calcium, phosphorus, and potassium, the heart-healthy minerals. Both the red and yellow watermelons have a high-water content of about 92 percent—equally tasty and pretty.

Fasting Drinks-Fluids

An herbal laxative tea can be a great helper for those who experience toxicity of their immune and other systems. It is good to take at the beginning of the master cleanse, both at night right before bedtime, and again, first thing in the morning.

For the sea saltwater drink, prepare a full quart of lukewarm purified water and add two level teaspoons of sea salt. Drink the

---

[6] Scinto, "Difference Between Red and Yellow."

quart of salt water first thing in the morning on an empty stomach. Within an hour, one to three eliminations will likely occur because the saltwater drink quickly and thoroughly washes out the entire digestive tract.

It is quite advisable to take the herb laxative tea at night to loosen the toxic waste, then the salt water each morning to wash it out. If for some reason the salt water cannot be taken in the morning or one chooses not to use it, then the herb laxative tea must be taken night and morning.

Herbal laxative tea or capsules work better at night because they help loosen the fecal matter to prepare the colon to eliminate it when the colon's energy is highest in the morning. Sea salt water or freshly juiced celery juice, which contains natural sodium, taken in the morning accentuates the colon's elimination. For those who choose not to drink the sea salt water or fresh celery juice, then the herbal laxative is suggested to take morning and night for maximum elimination.

Bone Broth

There are many amazing health benefits of bone broth during fasting and prayer.

Scientific research studies conducted on bone broth have found that it can improve your health in many different beneficial ways.

- Boosts immunity by supplying the amino acids that the body needs.

- Alleviates the common cold and bronchitis through the ages. Our grandmothers and their grandmothers have used bone broth in the form of chicken soup for years and it cleared up our common cold symptoms. In 2000 physicians found that there was solid scientific proof that chicken soup does indeed alleviate the common cold and bronchitis

- Bone broth fights inflammation. Other solid scientific studies show that the amino acids in bone broth have anti-inflammatory benefits, and specifically for the gut, our Microbiome.

- Bone broth strengthens bones and teeth. Another scientific study showed that the process of bone and teeth formation requires an adequate and constant supply of vitamins, minerals, and protein. Bone broth from grass fed meats and wild caught fish provides a good source of all these nutrients.

- Bone broth improves hydration. It adds electrolytes from minerals and carbohydrates from organic vegetables to a healthy diet. Scientific studies have shown that drinking broth can rehydrate better than water alone due to its electrolyte content. Do not disregard drinking purified water because the body is over 75 percent water, and it is a bare necessity of life.

- Build muscle with bone broth. The ten amino acids in bone broth can help stimulate muscle protein synthesis during fasting. Protein synthesis is essential for the continuous growth, repair, and maintenance of skeletal muscles. While researching I came across anecdotal evidence that shows that ingesting the amino acids, arginine, glutamine, cysteine, glycine, alanine, proline, hydroxyproline. cystine, histidine, and L-glutamine in bone broth helped stimulate protein synthesis and had anti-inflammatory properties.

In addition to those benefits of bone broth, the gelatin-rich protein that it contains has additional bonus side-benefits such as:

- Healthy strong nails
- Anti-aging properties
- Anti-tumor properties
- Arthritis and bone and joint-pain relief
- Cellular protection and repair
- Lower blood sugar in diabetes
- Regulates insulin
- Improves sleep quality
- Assists the body in regulating bleeding from nosebleeds, heavy menstrual flow, stomach ulcers, anal hemorrhoids, and bladder hemorrhage
- Helps normalize stomach acid, which is useful in the body healing itself of colitis, celiac disease, stomach ulcers, IBS, and other inflammatory digestive system conditions.

What about a Vegetarian's Broth?

If you are a vegetarian or vegan, you can make a broth, especially if you have a weakened digestive system. It can be the key to recovery because vegetables are easily broken down and absorbed.

If you eat healthy foods to feed your microbiome and your thoughts are positive, everything in your life works in a state of optimum health and wellness.

Both bone and vegetable broth are gentle ways to get important nutrients into the body. The whole process of making broth is one of the many pathways to loving and nourishing yourself through fasting and prayer.

Testimonials
Jody Richardson

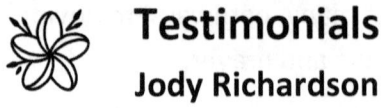

I remember a time in the mid-seventies when my college boyfriend and I had established a vegetarian house off campus. We rented rooms to vegetarians from Howard University and others in D.C. At some point some of us went to Dick Gregory's lecture on campus and decided to join in when he urged everyone to fast on Tuesdays and Fridays in political protest. I had done a few two-week fasts before and found it extremely enlightening, even euphoric. The bi-weekly fast did not feel the same but we continued to do it for a long time because we felt renewed.

A few years after we'd moved to Boston, I became Buddhist and learned to chant the prayer NAM-MYOHO-RENGE-KYO, which gave me instant access to my highest consciousness by praying for wisdom, the wellbeing of all, world peace, and focused manifestation. This gave my fasting more purposeful direction. So, through this discovery it taught me a valuable lesson and gave me lifelong purpose.

I have been enjoying this spiritual and natural health journey since 1971 when I began—voluntarily—fasting, so these details are what I remember about my fasting experiences. I can tell you that I've learned to respect nature's processes and to pay attention throughout.

Chapter Five:
Healthy Foods for Fasting

Health Benefits of Fruit and Vegetable Juices

In my almost forty years of practice, I have noticed that the following foods heal the body. This chapter is designed to give you some knowledge of these nutrient-dense foods. They are full of beneficial compounds and have the necessary elements that can nourish the body, balancing the systems and organs so they can achieve a level of optimum health and wellness. These essential vitamins, minerals, antioxidants, and other bioactive compounds have powerful medicinal properties. They help strengthen the body so that it will not develop many common preventable diseases, such as high blood pressure, diabetes, etc.

These foods can be used separately or in combinations. I prefer a combination because a combination of foods work better than just one. A single food can be added to the combination to accentuate its benefits. An example is carrot, apple, and ginger juice. If you add more carrots, that will accentuate its medicinal properties in the juice combination.

Apples

"An apple a day keeps the doctor away." This phrase was first coined in 1913 and was based on a Pembrokeshire proverb from 1866.

"Eat an apple on going to bed, and you'll keep the doctor from earning his bread." I have added to this famous phrase, "An apple a day keeps the doctor away...multiple apples a day will keep death at bay".

- Integrating apples into your diet helps to increase and maintain the optimum health of the cardiovascular, immune, skeletal, digestive, reproductive, brain, and nervous systems.

- Apples are beneficial for promoting the health of colon, heart, lungs, stomach and balancing the blood sugar. Also maintaining a healthy weight during and after weight loss, protects the brain against mental dysfunction and decline.

- Their nutritional components are high in antioxidants, flavonoids, pectin, potassium, and vitamin C. The apple's peel and seeds are also a rich source of fiber, vitamins, minerals, antioxidants, and protein.

Beets and Beet Greens

- Integrating beets and beet greens into your diet helps to increase and maintain the optimum health of the cardiovascular, immune, skeletal, digestive, reproductive, brain, and nervous systems.

- Beets and beet greens are beneficial for promoting the health of our eyes, colon, heart, lungs, stomach, skin, teeth and balancing the blood sugar. Also maintaining a healthy weight during and after weight loss and protects the brain against mental dysfunction and decline.

- Their nutritional components are high in folic acid, lutein, calcium, magnesium, vitamin A (as beta-carotene), B6, C, D, K, nitrates, iron, soluble and insoluble fiber.
- They are super prebiotics fibers that encourage the growth of healthy probiotics in the microbiome.

Bell Peppers

- Integrating bell peppers into your diet helps to increase and maintain the optimum health of the cardiovascular, immune, digestive, and respiratory systems.
- They are high in anti-inflammatory and anti-allergic properties. They have very powerful phenolics antioxidants, such as capsanthin, luteolin, and quercetin that are at a significantly higher level in the red pepper than the other colors. Nutritional components include folic acid, potassium, vitamin A (as beta-carotene), B6, C, E, K1, and soluble and insoluble fiber.
- Bell Peppers are beneficial for promoting the health of our eyes, heart, and stomach. Also maintains a healthy weight during and after weight loss, protects the brain against mental dysfunction and decline.

Cabbage

- Integrating cabbages into your diet helps to increase and maintain the optimum health of the cardiovascular, immune, and digestive systems.
- Cabbages are beneficial for promoting the health of our heart, liver, skin, hair, stomach, kidneys and balancing the

blood sugar. Also maintains a healthy weight during and after weight loss and protects the brain against mental dysfunction and decline.

- They are high in antioxidants. Nutritional components include folic acid, calcium, iron, magnesium, manganese, phosphorus, vitamin A, B, B6, Vitamin B2 (Riboflavin), C, K1, potassium, and prebiotic soluble and insoluble fiber.

- Anthocyanins, dietary flavonoids that reduce the risk factors of cardiovascular disease.

Carrots

- Integrating carrots into your diet helps to increase and maintain the optimum health of the cardiovascular, immune, skeletal, digestive, reproductive, brain, and nervous systems.

- Carrots are beneficial for promoting the health of our eyes, breast, colon, lungs, prostate, stomach and balancing the blood sugar. They are also important for our body's growth and the development of the brain during pregnancy and infancy.

- Their nutritional components are high in vitamins A (from alpha and beta carotene), B6, biotin, potassium, K1, lutein, lycopene, polyacetylenes, and anthocyanins.

Celery

- Integrating celery into your diet helps to increase and maintain the optimum health of the cardiovascular, immune, skeletal, digestive, reproductive, brain, and nervous systems.

- Celery is beneficial for promoting the health of our liver, colon, heart, lungs, stomach, skin, teeth and balancing the blood sugar. Also maintains a healthy weight during and after weight loss and protects the brain against mental dysfunction and decline.
- It is high in antioxidants and anti-inflammatory properties. Nutritional components include folic acid, lutein, calcium, magnesium, vitamin A (as beta-carotene), B6, C, D, K, nitrates, iron, potassium, and soluble and insoluble fiber.

Cucumber

- Integrating cucumbers into your diet helps to increase and maintain the optimum health of the cardiovascular, immune, digestive, skeletal, urinary, brain, and nervous systems.
- Cucumbers are beneficial for promoting the health of our heart, liver, skin, hair, stomach, kidneys and balancing the blood sugar. Also maintains a healthy weight during and after weight loss and protects the brain against mental dysfunction and decline.
- They are high in antioxidants, antimicrobial, and antiviral properties. Nutritional components include folic acid, calcium, choline, iron, lutein, magnesium, phosphorus, potassium, selenium, vitamin A, B, C, D, zeaxanthin, and soluble and insoluble fiber.

Ginger

- Integrating ginger into your diet helps to increase and maintain the optimum health of the cardiovascular,

- immune, skeletal, digestive, reproductive, brain, and nervous systems.
- Ginger is beneficial for promoting the health of our colon, heart, lungs, stomach, and balancing blood sugar. Also maintains a healthy weight during and after weight loss and protects the brain against mental dysfunction and decline.
- Its nutritional components are high in folic acid, iron, magnesium, niacin, phosphorus, potassium, riboflavin, zinc, vitamins B3, B6 and C.
- It is high in gingerol, "6-Gingerol" a major pharmacologically active pungent phenol that exhibits antioxidant, anti-tumor, anticancer, and anti-inflammatory properties.

Grapes

- Integrating grapes into your diet helps to increase and maintain the optimum health of the cardiovascular, immune, skeletal, digestive, reproductive, brain, and nervous systems.
- Grapes are beneficial for promoting the health of our eyes, colon, heart, lungs, stomach, skin, hair and balancing the blood sugar. Also maintains a healthy weight during and after weight loss and protects the brain against mental dysfunction and decline.
- They are high in antioxidants, anti-inflammatory, anti-aging, antimicrobial properties. Nutritional components include folic acid, lutein, calcium, copper, magnesium, manganese, riboflavin, thiamine, vitamin A (as beta-

carotene), B6, C, D, E, K, nitrates, iron, potassium, and soluble and insoluble fiber.

- They are high in melatonin for better sleep.
- Grapes are loaded with over 1,600 bioactive compounds. The dark red and purple grapes contain more antioxidants than white or green types and great for the root and crown chakras.

Grapefruits

- Integrating grapefruits into your diet helps to increase and maintain the optimum health of the cardiovascular, immune, skeletal, digestive, urinary, brain, and nervous systems.
- Grapefruits are beneficial for promoting the health of our colon, heart, lungs, stomach, skin, hair and balancing the blood sugar. Also maintains a healthy weight during and after weight loss and protects the brain against mental dysfunction and decline.
- They are high in antioxidants, anti-inflammatory, antimicrobial, antiviral properties, and phytochemicals. Nutritional components include vitamin A, C, potassium, and soluble and insoluble fiber.
- They increase the absorption of iron to prevent anemia.

Kale

- Integrating kale into your diet helps to increase and maintain the optimum health of the cardiovascular, immune, and digestive systems.

- Kale is beneficial for promoting the health of our eyes, liver, colon, heart, and stomach. Also maintains a healthy weight during and after weight loss and protects the brain against mental dysfunction and decline.
- Its nutritional components are high in folic acid, calcium, magnesium, manganese, vitamin A (as beta-carotene), B6, C, D, K, nitrates, iron, potassium, copper, and soluble and insoluble fiber.
- It is also very high in lutein, zeaxanthin, carotenoid antioxidants, and other powerful antioxidants (quercetin and kaempferol).
- Kale is king of all the super healthy greens. It is one of the most nutritious healthy plant foods on earth because of it being one of the best sources of vitamin K1.

Lemons

- Integrating lemons into your diet helps to increase and maintain the optimum health of the cardiovascular, immune, digestive, urinary, brain and nervous systems.
- Lemons are beneficial for promoting the health of our heart, liver, skin, hair, stomach, kidneys and balancing the blood sugar. Also maintains a healthy weight during and after weight loss and protects the brain against mental dysfunction and decline.
- They are high in antioxidants, anti-inflammatory, antimicrobial, and antiviral properties. Nutritional components include folic acid, calcium, choline, iron, lutein, magnesium, phosphorus, potassium, selenium, vitamin A, B, C, D, zeaxanthin, and soluble and insoluble fiber.

Lettuce

- Integrating lettuce into your diet helps to increase and maintain the optimum health of the cardiovascular, immune, digestive, skeletal, brain and nervous systems.

- It is high in anti-inflammatory properties. Nutritional components include folic acid, iron, lutein, phenolics, vitamin A (as beta-carotene), C, K1, soluble and insoluble fiber.

- Lettuce is beneficial for promoting the health of our eyes, heart, liver, skin, hair, stomach, kidneys and balancing the blood sugar. Also maintains a healthy weight during and after weight loss and protects the brain against mental dysfunction and decline.

Limes

- Integrating limes into your diet helps to increase and maintain the optimum health of the cardiovascular, immune, skeletal, digestive, urinary, brain and nervous systems.

- Limes are beneficial for promoting the health of our heart, lungs, and stomach, skin, hair and balancing the blood sugar. Also maintains a healthy weight during and after weight loss and protects the brain against mental dysfunction and decline.

- They are high in antioxidants, anti-inflammatory, antimicrobial, antiviral properties. Nutritional components include vitamin B, B1(thiamine), B6, C, potassium, and soluble and insoluble fiber.

Oranges

- Integrating Oranges into your diet helps to increase and maintain the optimum health of the cardiovascular, immune, skeletal, digestive, urinary, brain and nervous systems.

- Oranges are beneficial for promoting the health of our colon, heart, stomach, skin, and hair. Also maintains a healthy weight during and after weight loss and protects the brain against mental dysfunction and decline.

- They are high in antioxidants, anti-inflammatory, antimicrobial, and antiviral properties. Nutritional components include folic acid, calcium, magnesium, vitamin A, B, C, D, potassium, and soluble and insoluble fiber.

- They contain Hesperidin, a flavonoid antioxidant in their peel, and protects against Alzheimer's disease and reduces the risk factor of cancer.

- They help to produce collagen, increasing the absorption of iron to prevent anemia. Produce serotonin to promote happiness and good quality sleep.

Parsley

- Integrating parsley into your diet helps to increase and maintain the optimum health of the cardiovascular, immune, digestive, skeletal, and respiratory systems.

- It is rich in antioxidants; carotenoids, flavonoids, and has antibacterial properties. Nutritional components include folic acid, potassium, vitamin A, C, K, soluble and insoluble fiber.

- Parsley is beneficial for promoting the health of our eyes, heart, lungs, colon and balancing the blood sugar.

Pineapple

- Integrating pineapples into your diet helps to increase and maintain the optimum health of the immune, skeletal, and digestive systems.

- Pineapples are beneficial for promoting the health of our eyes, colon, heart, lungs, stomach, skin, hair and balancing the blood sugar. Also maintains a healthy weight during and after weight loss and protects the brain against mental dysfunction and decline.

- They are high in antioxidants, anti-inflammatory, anti-aging, and antimicrobial properties. Nutritional components include folic acid, lutein, calcium, copper, magnesium, manganese, vitamin A (as beta-carotene), B6, C, D, E, K, nitrates, iron, potassium, riboflavin, thiamine, and soluble and insoluble fiber. Also, bromelain for digestion.

Pomegranate

- Integrating pomegranates into your diet helps to increase and maintain the optimum health of the cardiovascular, immune, digestive, reproductive, skeletal, brain and nervous systems.

- They have punicalagins, an antioxidant that is three times more potent than green tea. They are antiviral and high in anti-inflammatory properties Their nutritional components include calcium, folic acid, potassium, C, K1, soluble and insoluble fiber.

- Pomegranates are beneficial for promoting the health of our prostate gland, eyes, heart, liver, skin, hair, stomach, kidneys and balancing the blood sugar. Also maintains a healthy weight during and after weight loss and protects the brain against mental dysfunction and decline.

- Anthocyanins and anthoxanthins, dietary flavonoids that reduce the risk factors of cardiovascular disease.

- They enhance athletes' performance, increase sexual performance, and is a powerful fertility booster.

Radishes and Tops

- Integrating radishes and tops into your diet helps to increase and maintain the optimum health of the cardiovascular, immune, digestive, skeletal, and respiratory systems.

- They are high in antioxidants, antibacterial and antiscorbutic properties. Nutritional components include calcium, copper, folic acid, iron, magnesium, manganese, niacin, phosphorus, potassium, riboflavin, sodium, and vitamin B-6, C, K, zinc, and soluble and insoluble fiber.

- Radishes and tops are beneficial for promoting the health of our heart, liver, lungs, stomach, colon, kidneys, bladder, skin and balancing the blood sugar. Also maintains a healthy weight during and after weight loss and protects the brain against mental dysfunction and decline.

Spinach

- Integrating spinach into your diet helps to increase and maintain the optimum health of the cardiovascular, immune, digestive, respiratory, skeletal, brain and nervous systems.

- It is high in anti-inflammatory properties. Nutritional components include calcium, folic acid, iron, lutein, magnesium, Manganese, phosphorus, vitamin A, B, B6, Vitamin B2 (Riboflavin), C, K1, and soluble and insoluble fiber.
- Spinach is beneficial for promoting the health of our eyes, heart, liver, skin, hair, stomach, kidneys and balancing the blood sugar. Also maintains a healthy weight during and after weight loss and protects the brain against mental dysfunction and decline.
- It is high in thylakoids that can reduce food cravings.

My Favorite Five Medicinal Juice Blend Recipes

Mix and match suggestions, directions, and amount of each.

Celery, Green Apple, Ginger, and Lemon

1 large bunch celery
4 green apples
1 thumb sized piece of ginger
1 small, peeled lemon

Carrots, Green Apple, and Ginger

12 large carrots
4 green apples
1 thumb sized piece of ginger

Celery, Green Apple, Ginger, and Lime

1 large bunch celery
4 green apples
1 thumb sized piece of ginger
1 small, peeled lime

Celery, Green Apple, Carrot, Ginger, Beet, and Parsley

1 large bunch celery
4 green apples
12 large carrots
1 thumb sized piece of ginger
2 large beets
1 bunch of parsley

Carrots, Green Apple, Ginger, and Kale

12 large carrots
4 green apples
1 thumb sized piece of ginger
1-2 bunch of kale

Very Important Contamination Information

Fruits and vegetables grown in contaminated soil or exposed to contaminated water may harbor larger amounts of heavy metals. This can affect their safety and quality. For your body to achieve optimum levels of health and wellness during your fasting and prayer journey, it is suggested to get and drink organic grown fruits and vegetables.

Testimonials
Michelle Vandepas

When I first heard about Intermittent fasting, I thought it would help me with weight loss, however what it really helped with was coughing, acid reflex, and indigestion issues. Giving my body a break between meals (NO Snacking!) was exactly what I needed to reset my body.

Asabi Carroll

My most memorable fast was not my own, but Dr. Jenkins godmother's. I was passing through Chicago and mom told me she was doing Dr. Jenkins supervised fast. She was so focused and determined, and each day she successfully completed the regiment he outlined for her, she became increasingly empowered.

I was amazed as I watched her prepare full meals for my father without taking a single bite, never wavering from the gallons of the herbal solution and the nature's sunshine tools he sent her home with. I saw her energy soar and her blood pressure, which we monitored daily, drop. She let nothing stop her, demanding that everyone respect her 8:00 a.m. yoga time with no disturbances. Those fourteen days changed her life and put her on a path that allowed her to impact everyone that she influenced.

Following Dr. Jenkins instructions for breaking her supervised fast helped her create the family traditions that we maintain now that she is a treasured ancestor. Several times weekly, mom washed and dried the ingredients for a massive salad. She lovingly chopped the vegetables and placed them in a huge plastic bowl with a lid. This allowed anyone visiting her kitchen at any time of the day or night to wash their hands and go to the Mama T salad bowl, which was always in place!

Chapter Six:
Healing the Body

The Rejuvenating Power of Fasting and Prayer on the body

During fasting and prayer, the healing is from the inside out and from the top down. A short to medium fast from one to seven days allows the body to rest, rejuvenate, and detoxify through a process called auto-detoxification (self-cleansing). This is the fastest and most powerful way of healing the mind, body, and spirit from disease.

I have told many people for years that as they continue to fast, their bodies go through a process called autolysis (self-eating). In this process the body consumes everything that is not necessary for bodily function, such as the fats as well as wasteful and diseased cells in a process called *autophagy*.

The physical, mental/emotional, and spiritual bodies have toxins being eliminated from them leading to healing during a combination of fasting and prayer.

The Physiological Changes

Many people lose their hunger in the first three to five days because their bodies are adjusting. That is a normal function that happens during periods of fasting. The primary source of energy for our bodies is sugar, but during this time it switches to fat stores as a source of energy.

When these fat stores are broken down, the physical, emotional, and spiritual chemical toxins are released. Each of these toxins will have different effects on your feelings. The heart with the lack of joy, stomach with worry, lungs with grief, large intestine with sadness, kidneys with fear, and the liver with anger and depression.

Recommendations for a Juice, Herbal Teas, and/or Water in a Fasting and Prayer Journey

- Transition from the Standard American Diet (SAD) of toxic, low nutrient dense foods into a cleansing raw food diet program for a period of fourteen to twenty-one days. Those people with chronic degenerative diseases such as high blood pressure, diabetes, or arthritis, just to name a few, should go on a cleansing semi-raw food diet program for up to ninety days. This can be done before, during, and after the fasting and prayer. This is one way they will get the best results.

- On a one to forty days of fasting and prayer consume a minimum of sixty-four ounces of freshly juiced organic fruit and veggie juices and if desire herbal teas. All freshly made juices must be diluted fifty-fifty with alkaline, mineral, spring, or distilled water. Do not use tap water, they have found hundreds of poisonous toxins in it. Do not do a forty day fast if you have never done a twenty-one day fast in your life.

- The break-fast period should be one day of breaking for every three to five days of fasting on juices or herbal tea by consuming fresh organic veggie broth soup and light to heavily steamed organic vegetables. Do one day of breaking the fast for every one to two days of water fasting. Because the digestive system is in a deeper sleep, it takes longer to wake it up and must be done carefully.

- For best results and a more positive eating lifestyle resume eating more of a plant-based diet with a seasonal raw food cleansing program for a better longer healthier life.

Returning to Normal After Your Deep Fasting and Prayer Cleanse

If your fast has been from ten to forty days, make sure to slowly reintroduce solid foods at least for four days, preferably a week for greater success. Be mindful and remember your breakfast is the most important part of fasting.

When you are finished with this period that you set aside for fasting and prayer, then you are ready to take food into your body again. It is most important to do so with great awareness. Make sure the foods you eat are nurturing your mind, body, spirit, and emotions.

Remember: Your microbiome, your digestive system, has stopped its normal function during your fast; it has been in a state of hibernation. It needs light organic foods at first so that it can slowly but surely re-start. As you take in veggie broth or freshly squeezed citrus juices, your microbiome begins to wake up again and function better than before. Digestive enzymes that are needed for the entire digestive system are starting to be produced again if you were greatly depleted prior to your fast. Your brain begins to use the nutrients from the healthy plant-based foods. All your body systems begin to perform at an optimum level of health and wellness. Allow your body to take all the time it needs to make these changes. Your fasting and prayer journey is a marathon not a sprint, so go slowly, one baby step at a time. The journey of a thousand miles starts with your first step. [7]

---

[7] Buhner, *Transformation Power of Fasting*.

Testimonials
Erica K Funchess

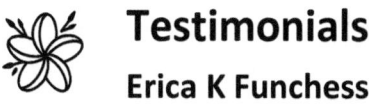

I started fasting for the first time in 2018 in preparation for a mission trip to Cuba. We started with eliminating one meal per day, then two meals, then twelve hours of fasting, and eventually to eighteen hours of fasting.

Because we eased into it, it was not that bad. I was nervous that I would not make it during the twelve-hour fast, but God helped me through it. I just made sure I drank plenty of water and stayed hydrated.

I prayed hard right before the eighteen-hour fast. God gave me renewed strength and courage as I prepared spiritually for an evangelism trip abroad. Despite getting very weak at times, especially when working and being very busy, I made it!

I am now motivated to fast regularly one day a week. We can do all things through Christ, who is the source of our strength.

"Then I heard the voice of the Lord, saying, 'Whom shall I send, and who will go for Us?' Then I said, 'Here am I. Send me!'"

Isaiah 6:8 NASB

Chapter Seven:
Healing the Mind and Emotions

Prayer is the Emotional Partner to Fasting

Your emotions control your overall health and your health controls your emotions. Mental, spiritual, and emotional stressors can create physical symptoms which can weaken the immune and other body systems, creating diseases. I had a patient that had a great deal of emotional stressors in her life from death of loved ones, loss of jobs, and other emotional stressors. Several years later she developed an autoimmune disease that created a lot of pain. The medication only managed the physical pain but never the root cause of the emotional pain.

History of Emotional Wellness Month

In our modern-day crazy stressful schedules, life is becoming more and more unpredictable. It is more vital than ever to maintain peace of mind, and balance of our emotional health and wellness.

A positive emotional self is important, and it must be maintained by making healthy choices in life. For us to achieve God's goal for our lives, we must have a positive relationship with family, friends, and community. Fasting and prayer gives us the strength of emotional wellness to handle the many stressors of life and to stay positively motivated.

Instead of worrying about the past and the future practice being in the present, where your body is, by using the meditative tradition of mindfulness. Move through life with peace and love for self. Rejecting the negative self-doubt that people try to put on you not just through fasting and prayer, but all through your rewarding life.

Did you know that your emotions are strongly affected by your lifestyle in such things like your sleeping habits and your diet? Poor quality sleep and bad diet affect the brain which is related to depression, anxiety, and other negative emotions. Getting seven to nine hours of good quality sleep and eating a healthy plant-based diet in addition to your fasting and prayer program can turn them around. "Love thy neighbor as thyself" but you must love yourself enough to love your neighbor. Are you able to process your feelings and handle those challenging times of life in a healthy and positive way?

The stressors of life have been associated with almost 100 percent of health issues. They can lead to chronic degenerative diseases like high blood pressure, headaches, diabetes, arthritis, and many others. If your life is so hard that you are not enjoying it, it is time to talk to your doctor or a therapist. Fasting and prayers added to your medical treatments can help you feel better than before both physically and spiritually. You will be more in tune with Father God, Mother Earth, and the Universe. A 2011 Harvard University Study showed that meditation and mindfulness can create new brain cells, which improves memory and cognitive functions. They have also been associated with lowering the risk factors to dementia and Alzheimer's disease.[8]

How to Celebrate Your Emotional Wellness on Your Fasting and Prayer Journey

The journey of fasting can be very demanding on the physical and mental bodies, but in conjunction with prayer, the journey can also be very rewarding. While fasting, consider adding to your routine some of the following.

- Gift yourself a much-needed essential oil massage.
- Fasting and Prayers as a community is beneficial to health and wellness. During your fasting and prayer journey, schedule some quality time with others. You all will benefit more from this extra support and love. "For where two or more have gathered in my name, I am there in their midst." Matthew 18:20 NASB2020
- Learn new coping skills, while fasting and praying. Take time to learn and develop a list of simple activities like deep abdominal breathing, yoga, qigong, meditation, and prayer that will help you calm down.

Visualization and Emotional Functions of Body Organs

Use these prompts to visualize the source of your emotions while praying. Understanding where your emotions "live" within your body will help you to work with them during a fast.

---

[8] "Emotional Wellness."

- Emotions start in our hearts and brains.
- The heart is the seat of emotions. and the brain is where they are processed.
- We feel emotions in our entire bodies.
- Our emotions control our health and our health controls our emotions. Chinese medicine states that each of the five elements have corresponding emotions and organs.
- Emotions are contagious. Studies have shown that humans unconsciously imitate the expressions and emotions of each others. Smiles can be contagious, but not fatal! Smiles can lead to laughter and laughter is the best medicine.
- Negative unpleasant emotions are very important to keep us in balance. To know how grateful we should be for the positive, pleasant emotions.
- Acknowledging negative emotions, releasing them, and immediately replacing them with positive emotions are very important to our health.

Prayers and Mantras That Will Help While Fasting

So, remove grief and anger from your heart and put away pain from your body, because childhood and the prime of life are fleeting."

Ecclesiastes 10:10 NASB2020
Additional resources Bible App****
Psalm 34:4NASB1995

"I sought the Lord, and he answered me; he delivered me from all my fears."

John 14:27NASB1995

"Peace I leave with you; my peace I give you. I do not give to you as the world gives. Do not let your hearts be troubled and do not be afraid."

Philippians 4:6-7NASB1995

[6] Be anxious for nothing; but in everything by prayer and supplication with thanksgiving let your requests be made known unto God. And the peace of God, which passeth all understanding, shall keep your hearts and minds through Christ.

"Cast all your anxiety on him because he cares for you."

"Now may the Lord of peace himself give you peace at all times and in every way. The Lord be with all of you."

"For ye have not received the spirit of bondage again to fear; but ye have received the Spirit of adoption, whereby we cry, Abba, Father."

"Search me, God, and know my heart; test me and know my anxious thoughts."

"The Lord himself goes before you and will be with you; he will never leave you nor forsake you. Do not be afraid; do not be discouraged."

For God did not give us a spirit of timidity or cowardice or fear, but He has given us a spirit of power, of love, and of sound judgment and personal discipline abilities that result in a calm, well-balanced mind and self-control.

2 Timothy 1:7NASB1995

Why Emotional Wellness Through Prayer is so Important

During our fasting and prayer journey, in addition to prayers we can incorporate affirmations and mantras which are gentle positive words and phrases. They change the way we think and move us into a state of self-love and self-worth.

"It takes a village to raise a child and it also takes a village to heal a body through Fasting and Prayers. Thank you, God, for our healing!"

This is my prayer to bless others.

 Testimonials
Shayda Biglari

"Fasting," said 'Abdu'l-Bahá "is the cause of awakening man. The heart becomes tender, and the spirituality of man increases. This is produced by the fact that man's thoughts will be confined to the commemoration of God, and through this awakening and stimulation surely ideal advancements follow".

The above statement is a great example of my own experience.

Within those 19 days of Baha'i fasting, from sunrise to sunset, I felt extremely closer to the Divine!

My soul and spirit became more & more purified.

At some point I feel very detached from this earthly world, although I'm proceeding with my daily tasks!

Most importantly fasting reminds me of hungry poor people in the world who would go hours without any food! Therefore, I try to provide more food and necessities for the needy since I feel their pain through starvation myself.

Like beloved Abdul-Baha has said, "My heart becomes tender."

Another interesting thing, my thoughts are always positive during fasting no matter how hard my days are.

Chapter Eight:
Healing the Spirit

Fasting and Prayer

Many sick people are reaching for health through man and not getting the result they seek. The answer to their healing questions is in God's healing therapies, fasting and prayer. People are always looking for a better way to live a long and healthier life but don't often realize the healing they seek can happen within themselves using these therapies.

Prayer and Mediation Quotes to Aid in Fasting

Use these prayers and meditations to help access the healing that comes from your fasting journey. There are prayers that I suggest for beginning your journey and ones for ending it. By creating structure to your fasts, you can increase your success and positive feelings while allowing God's healing to restore your health.

Opening Prayers and Mediations

Thy name is my healing, O my God, and remembrance of Thee is my remedy. Nearness to Thee is my hope, and love for Thee is my companion. Thy mercy to me is my healing and my succor in both this world and the world to come. Thou, verily, art the All-Bountiful, the All-Knowing, the All-Wise.

Baha'i Faith, Bahá'u'lláh

Beloved, I wish above all things that thou mayest prosper and be in health, even as thy soul prospereth.

Christianity, 3 John 1:2

Although ill health is one of the unavoidable conditions of man, truly it is hard to bear. The bounty of good health is the greatest of all gifts.

Baha'i Faith, Abdu'l-Baha

Engage thou in commemorating God at every morn …thy prevailing disease are not on account of sins, but they are to make thee despise this world and know that there is no rest and composure in this temporary life.

Bless the LORD, O my soul, and forget not all his benefits: Who forgiveth all thine iniquities; who healeth all thy diseases; Who redeemeth thy life from destruction; who crowneth thee with loving kindness and tender mercies; Who satisfieth thy mouth with good things; so that thy youth is renewed like the eagle's.

Christianity, Psalms 103:2-5

He healeth the broken in heart, and bindeth up their wounds.

Christianity, Psalms 147:3

Healing the Spirit

O Lord of the people! Remove the difficulty and bring about healing as You are the Healer. There is no healing but Your Healing...

Islam, Hadith, Bukhari Vol 7

There are two ways of healing sickness, material means and spiritual means. The first is by the use of remedies, or medicines; the second consists in praying to God and in turning to Him. Both means should be used and practiced.

Illness caused by physical accident should be treated with medical remedies; those which are due to spiritual causes disappear through spiritual means. Thus, an illness caused by affliction, fear, nervous impressions, will be healed by spiritual rather than by physical treatment. Hence, both kinds of remedies should be considered. Moreover, they are not contradictory, and thou shouldst accept the physical remedies as coming from the mercy and favor of God, who hath revealed and made manifest medical science so that His servants may profit from this kind of treatment also. Thou shouldst give equal attention to spiritual treatments, for they produce marvelous effects.

Baha'i Faith, Abdu'l-Baha

There is but one power which heals—that is God. The state or condition through which the healing takes place is the confidence of the heart. By some this state is reached through pills, powders, and physicians. By others through hygiene, fasting, and prayer.

Baha'iFaith, 'Abdu'l-Baha

Resort ye, in times of sickness, to competent physicians; We have not set aside the use of material means, rather have We confirmed it through this Pen, which God hath made to be the Dawning Place of His shining and glorious Cause…Well is it with the physician who cureth the ailments in My hallowed and dearly cherished Name.

             Baha'i Faith, Baha'u'llah

Be not wise in thine own eyes: fear the LORD and depart from evil. It shall be health to thy navel, and marrow to thy bones.

               Judaism, Proverbs 3:7,8

Beware of using any substance that induces sluggishness and torpor in the human temple and inflicted harm upon the body. We, verily, desire for you naught but what shall profit you, and to this bear witness all created things, had ye but ears to hear.

             Baha'i Faith, Baha'u'llah

But, if one deals with objects of the sense, Not loving and not hating, making them, Serve his free soul, which rests serenely lord, Lo! such a man comes to tranquility; And out of that tranquility shall rise, The end and healing of his earthly pains, Since the will governed sets the soul at peace.

               Hinduism, Bhagavad Gita

Four principal things increase in the man who is respectful and always honors his elders – length of life, good looks, happiness, and health.

       Buddhist, Dhammapada – Sayings of the Buddha 1

A merry heart doeth good like a medicine: but a broken spirit drieth the bones.

               Judaism, Proverbs 17:22

We should all visit the sick. When they are in sorrow and suffering, it is a real help and benefit to have a friend come. Happiness is a great healer to those who are ill...show the utmost kindness and compassion to the sick and suffering. This has greater effect than the remedy itself....

Baha'i Faith, `Abdu'l Bahá

Loose the bands of wickedness... undo the heavy burden... deal thy bread to the hungry... bring the poor that are cast out to thy house... When thou seest the naked cover him... Then... thine health shall spring forth speedily.

Christianity, Isaiah 58:6-8

If thou art desirous of health, wish thou health for serving the Kingdom. I hope thou mayest attain a perfect insight, an inflexible resolution, a complete health, and spiritual and physical strength in order that thou mayest drink from the fountain of eternal life and be assisted by the spirit of divine confirmation.

Baha'i Faith, `Abdu'l Bahá

Closing Prayers and Mediations

The book, *Healing Words*, by Sylvia Rogers gave me inspirations for this segment.

I wrote this book during the Covid-19 pandemic. The two most challenged body systems were the immune and digestive systems. The immune system because of the physical challenge from the Covid-19 virus itself and the emotional fear of the virus that weakened the immune system because of the low frequency of fear. The digestive system because of the "Covid Twenty", it is the same as the "Freshmen Fifteen" in college. So many people were inactive in doing physical activity and more active in doing food intake activity that the average person gain twenty plus pounds.

That overweight/obesity of the body is known to be a risk factor to Covid-19 and all other disease.

Prayers and Mediations for parts of the body

While fasting, speak aloud this prayer with intentions and convictions. It's all in God's time so take your time and visualize what you are praying for. God has given you authority through Christ because all things are possible through him.

Your Immune System

Dear Heavenly Father,

With the all-mighty name of Jesus, I will receive his words of healing that I am healthy and whole. It is written that if you ask it shall be given, so I ask that the following be eliminated from me down to my DNA:

- All forms of emotional and/or physical stressors, addictions of all types, medication toxicity and their side effects
- All absorbed radiation man made and/or environmental and all their side effects
- All toxic heavy metals, and their side effects.
- All chemicals and/or industrial pollutants from outside or inside sources of the house.
- All toxic environmental, and/or food allergens
- All bacteria, viruses, yeast, molds, and parasites, and any of their negative effects.
- With the faith of a mustard seed, I speak words of authority to those mountains and all their negative stories to be eliminated from me down to my DNA and never to return

for all eternity. This void that has been created must be filled with perfect health and wellness by the healing therapeutic powers of fasting and prayers.

I inhale with joy and peace your love and glory for my health and wellness and exhale all sickness and dis-ease. They are to cease anything negative to my health and wellness. Amen.

Your Digestive System

Dear Heavenly Father,

With the all-mighty name of Jesus, I will receive his words of healing that I am healthy and whole. It is written that if you ask it shall be given, so I ask that the following be eliminated from the DNA of my entire digestive system, from my mouth down to my anus:

- All forms of emotional and/or physical stressors, including a lack of feeling emotionally well fed and nourished, addictions of all types, medication toxicity and their side effects
- All lack of forgiveness, gratefulness towards God, others, and/or myself.
- All forms of digestive disorders including heartburn/acid reflux, nausea, vomiting, and sour stomach.
- In addition to fasting and prayers, I drink and eat with preservation, and strengthening of my digestive system. I dine peacefully with love, and joy for perfect digestion, absorption, circulation and elimination of God's healthy foods.

The wonderful healing remedies that fill me from the sole of my feet as I ground myself with Mother Nature to the top of my head as I connect with Father God, making me healthy and whole. I see myself living in optimum health and wellness as I praise your holy name. Amen.

Healing declarations

—use my chosen prayers from the bible I use. NASB1995 and/or NIV, that I know and will resonate with me and my million readers

I have used, throughout the years, the following scriptures that resonate with me off and on when God knows I need them.

The LORD is my light and my salvation— whom shall, I fear? The LORD is the stronghold of my life— of whom shall I be afraid? (Psalm 27:1 NIV)]

And without faith it is impossible to please God, because anyone who comes to him must believe that he exists and that he rewards those who earnestly seek him. (Hebrews 11:6 NIV)]

No weapon forged against you will prevail, and you will refute every tongue that accuses you. (Isaiah 54:17 NIV)]

Death and life are in the power of the tongue, and those who love it will eat its fruit. (Proverbs 18:21 NASB 1995]

Don't allow any man, woman, especially any doctor to talk death into your life. No matter if you have a chronic heart disease, chronic kidney failure, any other chronic degenerative diseases, forth stage cancer, or even any infectious pandemic virus. **With the power of your own tongue and the faith in God through fasting and prayer, you and he can heal all diseases of his earthly temple.**

Remove grief, anger, depression, other negative emotions, and especially all fears from your heart and put away pain from your body, because childhood and the prime of life are fleeting.

Testimomials

Christopher F. Smith

I've been sick for almost fifteen years and this extremely powerful prayer along with fasting and Tai Chi Chuan has changed my life. My biological time clock is slowing down and I'm getting younger and stronger. I'm seventy-years-old and a Vietnam veteran. I spend a lot of time in the Garden of Eden. Thank you, My Lord Jesus Christ for All of Your Help.

Debbie Perez-Cockburn

Before I fast, I ponder the things I would like Heavenly Father's answers to or to get help with. I spend the next twenty-four hours abstaining from food and drink and spend it in prayer and meditation. I put aside a generous amount of money I would have spent on eating out and give that as an offering to my Bishop to be used for the needy in our congregation. I find that when I truly pray with strength of heart, mind, and soul I feel inspired and find answers to my prayers. I feel lifted and can forget my cares as I dedicate myself to a higher purpose.

Chapter Nine:
What to Expect When Healing

Healing and the Physical Crises

You May be Experiencing a Physical Healing Crisis.[9]

Do you know what a Healing Crisis is and/or have you ever experienced one? It is not uncommon for people to experience a cleansing and detoxification reaction when they begin a health and wellness program. This is called a healing crisis; it occurs when the body is recycling toxins. It is a normal process that people may encounter on their path to health and wellness, especially if they have chronic diseases.

"Herxheimer Reaction" is the medical term for the healing crisis. It occurs when the body is detoxifying and releasing toxins from the cells into the body by the organs of elimination. These organs: lungs, colon, kidneys & bladder, circulation & lymphatics, liver, and skin are not able to eliminate them fast enough. Those

---

[9] Jockers, "Healing Crisis."

toxins that remain in circulation can affect all the body's organs, especially the brain leading to nausea, poor coordination, headaches, fatigue, brain fog, decreased cognition, fever, etc. (1, 2).

"Die-Off" and the Healing Crisis

Die-Off is a process caused by the body from a sudden increase in endotoxins. These endotoxins are harmful substances that are released when microorganisms such as fungi, yeasts, bacteria, and viruses are destroyed and die off. This rapid death of the microorganisms can cause a flood of endotoxins into the system.

An Inflammatory reaction triggers an acute immune response that can be experienced throughout the body. This leads to chronic symptoms of all health issues, as the development of new symptoms.

Die-off is commonly the result of side effects of medications such as antifungals, antibiotics, and others. Many people don't know that when they change their diets during a cleansing detoxification program or start eating healthier, they can possibly experience die-off and its symptoms

Common Symptoms of Die-off: Bloating and /or gas, brain fog, constipation or diarrhea, fatigue, flu-like symptoms, headaches, irritability and moodiness, joint aches and pains, nausea, and skin issues.

The Physical Healing Crisis is a Natural & Healthy Process

The healing crisis is a very natural process and unique to each individual person. Most people experience mild symptoms while others may experience severe ones. Understanding these symptoms are only temporary and will subside within a few days because the body gets cleaner and is able to eliminate more toxins. These symptoms usually reduce within two to seven days, occasionally in the person who is toxic it may last a few weeks.

People need to understand that a holistic health is not harming them during their healing crisis experience. They should not negatively think of a positive experience, but pain and discomfort make people feel that way. The years and years of store toxins and accumulate pathogens develop chronic diseases faster.

People suffering from major diseases and/or developing other diseases, may experience new symptoms with more extreme reactions during a healing crisis. On occasion the crisis will come after the individual feels at their very best or after a cleansing detoxification program. They will feel on top of the world and the healing crisis may hit them hard the next day. The most common symptoms may include nausea, vomiting, diarrhea, night sweats, hot or cold flashes, increased blood pressure, headaches, joint pain, and fatigue just to name a few of the many other symptoms.

Respiratory healing crisis example: The Healing crisis can look just like a disease crisis. If one does not know the difference, they may end up in the emergency room or their doctor's office. A respiratory disease crisis may look like a cold to the flu to bronchitis to asthma to emphysema to COPD then possibly lung cancer. A respiratory healing crisis is the reverse to a disease crisis and goes from lung cancer to COPD to emphysema to asthma to bronchitis to the flu and then to the cold, but the symptoms look the same. That's why it's important to be monitored by a healthcare practitioner who is knowledgeable of the healing crisis.

Fasting and Prayer to Cleanse the Body

Fasting and prayer are common strategies used to cleanse the body and are often associated with the healing crisis. During this time, the energy and blood is rerouted from the digestive system to other areas of the body where it can now be used for cleansing, building, and healing.

Everyone should use these strategies periodically to improve and maintain cellular health and wellness. Many people choose to do a three-to-seven-day cleansing diet prior to their fasting and prayer program every quarter. While others, like myself, choose to do a twenty-four to thirty-six hour weekly fasting and three days per month fast.

During a fast, the best way to minimize the healing crisis symptoms is to incorporate drinking freshly juiced fruit and veggie juices that are rich in vitamins, minerals, enzymes, prebiotics, and probiotics to enhance the cleansing process. Some of the best fruit and veggie juices to include in a cleansing program are carrot, green apple, ginger, beets with the beet greens, celery, lemon, and kale just to name a few.

Tips for Handling a Healing Crisis:

- Super hydrate your body: Since the body is 70 to 75 percent water, it is the best fluid to flush toxins out of the body. Be sure to drink at least half your bodyweight in ounces of water. A great recommendation is to drink two to four ounces every fifteen minutes that you are awake to super hydrate your body and to flush out the endotoxins and inflammatory agents. The best water to use is filtered, spring, distilled, and alkaline water.
- Use lemon and raw honey in your water: Lemon and raw honey help to alkalize your body and flush out the

endotoxins, enhance detoxification, neutralize free radicals, and heal the inflammatory damage. For a gallon of water use the juice of four fresh lemons and raw honey to taste.

- Essential oils-single and blends: Essential oils have the highest energy of any of God's medicine. There are over eighty-eight passages in the bible about essential oils. Many of them like frankincense, lavender, atlas cedar, orange, peppermint, and ylang ylang have relaxing and calming properties. These powerful oils are fantastic to eliminate the healing crisis symptoms. The best way to use them is either directly inhaling them, using a diffuser, mixing with a carrier oil, applying topically, or in a very relaxing bath with Epsom salt, baking soda with some ginger powder.

- Get good quality sleep as much as possible: Sleep is a very critical part of your healing and detoxification process. It is highly recommended during a healing crisis to sleep between ten to twelve hours a night. The benefits of getting a full night's rest are to boost your immune system, strengthen your heart, help your energy levels soar to lead to loving healthy moods, increase brain productivity to improve concentration, memory, and higher cognitive function.

- Bulk up on probiotics: Healthy probiotic microorganisms help to detoxify the endotoxins and improve gut motility. It is best to use a non-GMO, dairy free probiotic with between ten to twenty strains and fifteen to twenty billion CFU. I have suggested to some of my clients to take two to three times as much as suggested on the bottle during their healing crisis.

- Use bone broth and/or collagen: These healing supplements help to improve the immune system, reduce inflammation, and heal a leaky gut. You can buy or make organic chicken, beef, or vegetable broth and drink throughout the day during the healing crisis and during your fasting and prayer.

- Use bitter herbs: In TCM, the wood element organs are the liver and gallbladder, and the taste is bitter. Bitter herbs and foods feed and strengthen the liver and gallbladder. Commonly used bitter herbs are cilantro, dandelion, ginger, milk thistle, and parsley, which all have powerful liver and gallbladder cleansing detoxification properties.

- Use onion, garlic, and ginger tea: The sulfur in the onion is a very effective anti-inflammatory. It also lowers the blood pressure and reduces the risk of heart attacks. The antioxidants it contains come from the polyphenols, that fight against free radicals that are known to harm the body. The sulfur in the garlic is very effective against endotoxins and the toxicity of heavy metals, such as lead, mercury, aluminum and others that can harm the body. The properties of ginger such as its strong anti-inflammatory, anti-parasitic, antiviral and antibacterial properties make it one of the most powerful foods for many centuries.

- See your naturopathic doctor, chiropractor, or another natural health practitioner. The excessive endotoxin inflammation causes tremendous stress on the body's organ systems. It is important to enhance the function of them for the cleansing and detoxification processes to be at their most efficient level. Have your doctor check you three times a week if not daily while you are going through the healing crisis.

- Use activated charcoal and psyllium hulls: They give unparalleled support for a full body cleansing and elimination, healthy intestinal lining integrity, and heavy metal detoxification.

Healing and the Spiritual Crises

Ways to Guide You Through a Spiritual Healing Crisis.[10]

The spiritual healing crisis is a time in your life where you may experience intense emotional healing and release. It may occur after emotional healing therapies or spiritual counseling sessions. It can also occur after Qigong or Reiki energy treatments. A healing crisis can result as a significant shift in your beliefs from a negative mindset to a positive one of yourself.

In your life you may have experienced your own spiritual healing crisis. Here is a list of common symptoms, if you are not sure that you have gone through one:

- Fatigue, lethargy, sleepiness, and tiredness
- Lack of doing anything or motivation
- Lack of focus, "brain fog"
- Dizziness, headaches, vertigo
- Return of aches and pains throughout the body
- Emotionally crying for no reason whatsoever
- A sense of grief, loss, sadness, depression, anxiety, or any other negative emotion
- Mental confusion or lack of sense of direction

---

[10] Hardman, "Spiritual Healing Crisis."

- Your life just seen to be falling apart
- Lost enjoyment in your previous activities, hobbies, or interests
- Feeling intensely emotionally angered, frustrated, and grieved for no reason whatsoever
- Craving salty, sugary, and fatty foods
- Indifference in foods or no appetite

In a real spiritual healing crisis, these symptoms will lessen in intensity and then disappear. Anytime these symptoms get worse, it may be something else. Get them checked out by a naturopathic doctor, chiropractor, or other natural health practitioner.

When our spiritual lives get deeper with God, a spiritual healing crisis is almost inevitable. Being uncomfortable while it happens is an external sign that our mindset is shifting to a positive lifestyle.

Here are some techniques you can use to reduce the intensity and length of the healing crisis. You get out of it what you put into it, so you must go through it to become spiritually stronger. Like they say, "If you are going through hell, just keep going."

- Reduce the intensity of your mental/emotional work such as spiritual counseling, DreamWorks, hypnotherapy, past life works, psychotherapy, etc.
- Increase your forms of self-care with affirmations, grounding, meditation, yoga, Qigong, quality sleep, and prayers. These practices will unblock, balance, and heal your chakras and other energy fields.
- Regular alkalizing detox bath with Epsom salt, baking soda, essential oils, and soaking for a minimum of twenty

minutes. You may have an emotional and physical release into the water.

- Have a self-care day by taking a day off from work, kids, family, and everything else. Do for yourself, it is the best therapy you can ever get. Turn off all electronics because they negatively affect your healing crisis.

- It is important to stay in communication with your fasting and prayer community of accountability partners, friends, and/or mentors. As you are going through things let them know, they are there to support you. We are or have all gone through these in our lives. During your fasting and prayer journey, these spiritual healing crisis experiences are normal, natural and to be expected.

- Make time for yourself by saying yes to yourself instead the many yeses you say to others. That will add so much to your already plate that it is as full as a platter. It needs to be emptied so that you can take a deep breath to recharge, revitalize and rejuvenate.

- Use spiritual or psychic tools. If you are into Angel cards, crystals, pendulums, or Tarot cards, this is the perfect time to use them. Write in a journal the ideas and insights that come to you about your healing crisis. Ask yourself is this a true healing crisis that I must go through, what am I to learn from it? Is it something that I am supposed to learn to make me better? Writing things down helps to get them out of your head to release that negative energy to make you better.

- And don't forget to smile!

Testimonials

Charrice Miller

Fasting and prayer helped me build my confidence, strength, and my spiritual connection with the creator. The ability to control my appetite for food is like an addict quitting "cold turkey" to kick a drug habit. It takes commitment, vision, faith, and prayer to overlook the urge not to break my fast. Once I overcame my urges to eat, I gained strength and confidence to battle through. When I started seeing the results, such as beautiful glowing skin, weight lost, and a clear mind, I knew I won the war. I was victorious by overcoming the flesh and graduating to a new level of consciousness and understanding of self.

Allene Shields

Initially, I went on a fast to detox my body to lose a few pounds. I was never concerned that I was taking blood pressure medication (Norvase) for high blood pressure with all the side effects, such as headache, edema, lightness, and` palpitations to name a few. I never got enough sleep, but I just related that to my job. I would leave the television on to put me to sleep and take meds for my sinuses. So, I went on a fast for one week. Dr. Jenkins supplied a detox tea, and I ate fruits, veggie, protein, and then no food after six or seven p.m. I drank half my body weight in ounces of water and lost six or seven pounds. That next week I fasted every other day and began meditating to focus on the mind. I noticed I stopped craving junk foods, slept better, and was altogether feeling great. I went for my annual checkup and my blood pressure was down with no medication.

Chapter Ten:
Twenty-One-Day Devotional

Your Fasting and Prayer Devotional Journey

Now that you have read this book on fasting and prayer, I put them together for you to see their ultimate powers. You can add them to your lifestyle to see the many blessings and glory that God has revealed within you.

Day 1

Description: Fasting and prayer are not just going without food, or a spiritual battle, or a discipline, or therapies to get your wants and needs from God. They are a spiritual journey that may lead you to a new place physically, mentally, and emotionally but primarily leads you to a new spiritual place.

Scripture: Then, when they had fasted and prayed and laid their hands on them, they sent them away. (Acts 13:3 NASB 1995)

Challenge: If you have never fasted and prayed together a day in your life and you feel, no know in your heart that something great is missing in your life, than take that leap of faith. Without faith it is impossible to please God and if you take that first step, he will take two.

Day 2

Description: Fasting is more than just missing a meal for an hour, a day, a week, or even a month. It is sacrificing something of a lesser value to acquire something of a much higher value, God's great grace and mercy. The many seasons of powerful fasting are experienced when we propose to spend quality time in God's presence in prayer during the fast. More than just the hunger pangs, fatigue, and withdrawal headaches, these are just a few of the many reminders to call on the Lord our God. Fasting and prayer are desperate measures for those desperate for God.

Scripture: Who is the King of glory? The Lord strong and mighty, The Lord mighty in *battle*. (Psalms 24:8 NASB 1995)

Challenge: As you start fasting, understand that you have entered a battle that is spiritual, mental, physical, and emotional. Part of this battle is fought as the body adjusts to the fasting rigors. There is more than just cleansing and detoxification going on in our bodies. This battle is more than physiological and mental, as we fast, a spiritual and emotional battle is being waged more so. God reveals to us in the spiritual realm things are happening that we neither perceive nor understand.

Day 3

Description: Delight yourself in the Lord through fasting and prayer and he will give you the healthy heart you desire, not just the physical heart but also the emotional heart which is the seat of all emotions. The Lord is my light thru prayer and my salvation thru fasting. I shall fear no evil because my faith in God is stronger than fear.

Scripture: Delight yourself in the Lord; And He will give you the desires of your heart (Psalms 37:4 NASB 1995)

The LORD is my light and my salvation; Whom shall, I fear? The LORD is the defense of my life; Whom shall I dread? (Psalms 27:1 NASB1995)

Challenge: *What* are you needing and wanting God to do through your days of fasting and prayer? What are your fasting and prayers for? Write your goals down in a journal and look at them daily as you pray. When your hunger or cravings come, read your goals out loud to remind yourself that your fasting and prayers are for a purpose. Through your fasting and prayer journey, God will always answer your prayers, he never fails! When God's people fast and pray, the supernatural happens.

Day 4

Description: In our lives, God will do some things only in response to us spending time in fasting and prayer to be in his presence. They liberate people to break the strongholds that move us into realizing God's power within us. The more time spent with God through fasting and praying, the more of God's miracles you are going to see in your life and the lives of others.

Scripture: 17A man in the crowd answered, "Teacher, I brought you my son, who is possessed by a spirit that has robbed him of speech. 18Whenever it seizes him, it throws him to the ground. He foams at the mouth, gnashes his teeth and becomes rigid. I asked your disciples to drive out the spirit, but they could not."19 "You unbelieving generation," Jesus replied, "how long shall I stay with you? How long shall I put up with you? Bring the boy to me."

23"'If you can'?" said Jesus. "Everything is possible for one who believes." 24Immediately the boy's father exclaimed, "I do believe; help me overcome my unbelief!" 28After Jesus had gone indoors, his disciples asked him privately, "Why couldn't we drive it out?" 29He replied, "This kind can come out only by prayer. (Mark 9:17-19, 23-24, 28-29 NIV)

Challenge: There may be many obstacles of your mind, body, spirit, and emotions that you have been facing for a very long time. Perhaps you have prayed and asked others to pray for you, and you do not understand why you are not making any forward process. You are probably thinking and praying, will God ever give me peace. Somethings only come by fasting and prayer.

Day 5

Description: We may be facing situations that are testing our courage and strength, through fasting and prayer we believe God is going to use them to bring his blessings into our life.

Scripture: No temptation has overtaken you except something common to mankind; and God is faithful, so He will not allow you to be tempted beyond what you are able, but with the temptation will provide the way of escape also, so that you will be able to endure it. (1 Corinthians 10:13 NASB2020)

Challenge: We asked God for his blessings in our life challenges, and we must deny our stomachs for the purpose of showing that our desires and needs for God's help are greater than our desires and needs for food.

Day 6

Description: Fasting and prayer bring mental clarity, self-confidence, and personal commitment to make it through your seasons of change. During fasting and prayer, the use of essential oils brings powerful anointing for these new seasons of life.

Scripture: So, he (Moses) was there with the Lord for forty days and forty nights; he did not eat bread or drink water. And He wrote on the tablets the words of the covenant, the Ten Commandments. (Exodus 34:28 NASB 1995)

While they were serving the Lord and fasting, the Holy Spirit said, "Set Barnabas and Saul apart for Me for the work to which I have called them." Then, when they had fasted, prayed, and laid their hands on them, they sent them away (Acts 13:2-3 NASB1995).

Challenge: Winter, Spring, Summer, and Fall –just as the external seasons change so do our internal seasons with every other aspect of our lives. Even though we must accept these seasonal changes are constant, it does not mean it is easy. Resistance makes us stronger. Life changes always bring excitement and uncertainty as we try to accept these new opportunities or challenges, we face. That is why fasting, and prayer are so important during seasons of transition and change. Looking through Scripture, we see the new seasons of God's blessings and works are always preceded by fasting and prayer.

Day 7

Description: The many constant earthly distractions that surround us daily can and do block our ability to hear God. Everything up to and including social media distract us from hearing God clearly. The fasting and praying seasons help quiet our hearts so we can hear spiritually from him. There is the ultimate spiritual high that comes through and from fasting and prayer.

Scripture: But if the distance is so great for you that you are not able to bring the tithe, since the place where the LORD your God chooses to set His name is too far away from you when the LORD your God blesses you (Deuteronomy 14:24 NASB1995)

Challenge: Have you felt a great distance from God, feeling that you were in a spiritual desert? You are praying to God, but it seems that your prayers are falling on deaf ears. You might be thinking, "Why is not God responding to me, please God forgive me?" Your best question should be, "Why is God's voice being blocked in my life?" If you are struggling to hear God's voice, you may be blocking your own blessings with your own unkind negative attitude so one of the best things you must do is regularly fast and pray.

Day 8

Description: As we fast one of the most important things, we can do is to spend time praying and praising God. Do not just pray about your problem, praise God knowing that he is solving problems. The Lord is faithful to fight for you in whatever battles you are facing, as you look to him and praise him.

Scripture: And he said, "Listen, all you of Judah and the inhabitants of Jerusalem, and King Jehoshaphat: This is what the Lord says to you: 'Do not fear or be dismayed because of this great multitude, for the battle is not yours but God's. (2 Chronicles 20:15 NASB1995)

Challenge: All of us will have battles of our mind, body, spirit, and emotions in our lives. The question is how will we react to these battles? In response to God's people fasting, he encourages us by saying, whatever we are facing, depends on our Heavenly Father because he is faithful to go before us. God shows up, fights our battles, and always wins!

Day 9

Description: You are now on day nine of your fast and you have conquered the hunger challenge of days three or four. What you were hungry and craving for was not just physical but also mental, emotional, and spiritual. It's not just craving foods but also social media, TV bingeing, and other things that are wasting your mind and blocking you from moving forward in life. Fasting is all about craving the appetite of spiritual consciousness through prayer.

Scripture: 30and Esau said to Jacob, "Please let me have a swallow of that red stuff there, for I am famished." Therefore, his name was called Edom. 31But Jacob said, "First sell me your birthright." 32Esau said, "Behold, I am about to die; so of what *use* then is the birthright to me?" (Genesis 25:30-32NASB1995)

Challenge: Are you willing to sacrifice something of a lesser quality to acquire something of a much greater quality that your craving can never give you? Would you be like Esau and sell your birthrights of health, wealth, and prosperity which is of a higher value for a single meal which is of lesser value.

Day 10

Description: A key part of fasting and prayer is giving considerable time to waiting on God, be still and let God. When you spend time in God's presence, he will reveal things beyond your imagination. They are not just about getting what we want or about what God wants to do for us in our lives. No, it is about hearing from him.

There are things that God wants to do in our lives through fasting and prayer. He will give you the self-confidence you need to start that new business or take your next business to the next level or rebuild your relationships with spouse, family, friends, and others.

He may tell you not to take that step even if you feel it is a sure thing. He may ask you to wait on him a bit longer or not to do it all. Part of spiritual maturity that you earn thru fasting and prayer is being able to understand what God is saying, and act on it.

Scripture: Yet those who wait for the LORD Will gain new strength; They will mount up with wings like eagles, they will run and not get tired, they will walk and not become weary. (Isaiah 40:31 NASB1995)

Challenge: Everything is in God's time not ours. As you are fasting and praying today, ask God to speak to you and just listen to his wisdom for your life.

Day 11

Description: God's love is to do new and great things in our lives, yet we see our future through the eyes of our past. As wise people, we learn from our mistakes and grow from our failures. If we do not learn from our mistakes and failures, we are allowing those past disappointments to blind us from seeing God's promises in us.

Maybe you have been praying for God to move some situations in your life. You may believe it is possible for God to grant all promises, but you do not have the faith that his promises are possible for you. God's promises are for all, you just must have the faith and belief.

Scripture: For I do not wish to see you now just in passing; for I hope to remain with you for some time, if the Lord permits. (1 Corinthians 16:7 NASB1995)

Challenge: God wants you to experience something wonderful and new in your life. He wants to bring forth growth, beauty, vitality, and longevity to his temple that you have been living in. He made a way where there is no way if you walk by faith and not by sight through fasting and prayer, you will see his way.

Those days of fasting and prayer will lead to new and wonderful experiences in and around you as you are being honored by the Lord. Watch and anticipate his greatness, you may not see it now, but it's impossible to fast and pray without seeing God's work in response to our faith in Him.

Day 12

Description: When God is all, you realize through fasting and prayer that God will supply all your needs according to his riches and glory. Jesus said, "Seek first the kingdom of God and His righteousness and all these other things will be given to you."

Scripture: And He sent them out to proclaim the kingdom of God and to perform healing. (Luke 9:2 NASB1995)

for *the kingdom of God* is not eating and drinking, but righteousness and peace and joy in *the* Holy Spirit. (Romans 14:17NASB1995)

Challenge: Our goals and desires determine the course of our lives. What we want or what wants us. Our goals and desires determine what we do, search for, and how we think. What are our goals and desires for our future lives?

As we continue fasting and prayers, they will help us to seek God as the number one priority in our life. The ultimate of what we need is to grow closer in our walk with God to be able to achieve our optimum level of Health and Wellness.

Day 13

Description: Daniel fasted for three weeks from the king's rich diet of sweets, meats, alcohol, and more. During his twenty-one days he also prayed, it appeared to him that nothing had happened! Daniel did not see or hear anything until the twenty-fourth day which was his break-fast period, but the answers to his fasting and prayer journey were on their way from the very first day of his fast.

Scripture: "In the third year of Cyrus king of Persia, a revelation was given to Daniel...it concerned a great war. At that time, I, Daniel, mourned for three weeks. I ate no choice food; no meat or wine touched my lips; and I used no lotions at all until the three weeks were over. On the twenty-fourth day of the first month..." (Daniel 10:1-4a NIV).

"Then he continued, 'Do not be afraid, Daniel. Since the first day that you set your mind to gain understanding and to humble yourself before your God, your words were heard, and I have come in response to them'." (Daniel 10:12 NIV)

Challenge: When you fast and pray, your heavenly angels and God take note. It may not seem like anything is happening, but the moment you begin your fasting and prayer journey, God has been working on your mind, body, spirit, and emotions. Do not quit fasting and praying. Do not stop looking within yourself what God has for you. Continue your journey with the faith and expectation that you will see God do extraordinary miracles in your life.

Day 14

Description: There is nothing like fasting and prayer to remind you of where your weaknesses and your real strengths are found. Your strength comes straight from your God from within. Many times, in our lives, all of us come under the illusion that we have what it takes to handle whatever comes our way, but seasons of fasting and prayer remind us that only through dependence on God can we truly overcome those challenges of life. I can do all things through Christ who strengthens me.

Scripture: "Now therefore, our God, the great God, mighty and awesome, who keeps his covenant of love, do not let all this hardship seem trifling in *your* eyes—the hardship that has *come* on us, on our kings and leaders, on our priests and prophets, on our ancestors and all *your* people, *from* the days of the kings of Assyria until today. (Nehemiah 9:32 NIV)

Challenge: God has all the strength you need. Seek him and you will feel his strength flow in and through your life in a new dynamic way. As you continue your fasting and prayer journey be encouraged that though you may feel weak at the beginning, he is empowering you to become stronger.

Day 15

Description: We as God's people are on a journey to optimum health and wellness. Rather than approaching man to help with these matters of sickness, we believe the Lord our God will come through, so he called us to fast and pray. God responded to our faithful fasting and prayers, protecting us from disease of the mind, body, spirit, and emotions. When we fast and pray, God opens doors that would otherwise be closed just by praying. We can have confidence that God will meet our needs as we call to him. God loves to show up and show out his grace and mercy during our needs.

Scripture: And my God will supply all your needs according to His riches in glory in Christ Jesus. (Philippians 4:19 NASB1995)

Challenge: Take all your wants and needs to God, your needs more than your wants. Knowing and believing through faith that he hears all your prayers. Be still and wait on God, as he performs impossible miracles because that is what he does. Then I proclaimed that we ground ourselves as we are fasting and praying either in a live body of water, or on bare ground that we might humble ourselves before God. Seeking from him a safe journey to health and wellness for ourselves, our little ones, our elders, and all in our community.

Day 16

Description: The freshness we long for and the strength we need in our lives begins with us being in the presence of God. Ask God to fill you with fresh faith, fresh passion, fresh enthusiasm, and fresh perspective, and then watch that freshness spills out into everything you do. During our days of fasting and prayer, take time to wait on God and he will bring into your life freshness.

Scripture: And do not be conformed to this world, but be transformed by the renewing of your mind, so that you may prove what the will of God is, that which is good and acceptable and perfect. (Romans 12:2 NASB1995) Yet those who wait for the LORD Will gain new strength; They will mount up *with* wings like eagles, they will run and not get tired, They will walk and not become weary. (Isaiah 40:31 NASB1995)

Challenge: Given a choice, most people want freshness now: fresh food and drinks, fresh unpolluted air, fresh ideas, fresh perspective on life, or fresh faith in God—it is just better. But freshness in your spiritual life doesn't happen automatically or by accident; it must be cultivated: seed time and harvest. Fake pathways to internal freshness are advertised all the time, yet the real thing only comes one way by fasting and prayer.

Day 17

Description: With the positive and/or negative thoughts we make daily, it is interesting that there are well over 60,000 of them. We also make thousands of positive and/or negative decisions, there are also well over 35,000 of them. Sometimes your process of decisions is made by your subconscious mind while you are sleeping from the previous day's activities and thoughts. We need to never stop fasting and prayer throughout our lives to concentrate on the positive thoughts, feelings, and decisions so that we can acquire the valuable insights into fulfilling God's will in our lives.

Scripture: Seven days you shall celebrate a feast to the LORD your God in the place which the LORD chooses, because the LORD your God will bless you in all your produce and in all the work of your hands, so that you will be altogether joyful. (Deuteronomy 16:15 NASB1995)

Challenge: When we choose to continually fast and pray throughout our lives, we realign our thoughts and our priorities in a way that directly affects our decisions. God cares how we spend our time and energy. So, pray for the presence of the Lord to precede your every move.

In our 60,000 plus thoughts and 35,000 decisions we make daily, make prayer a priority and invite God's direction into every thought and movement of your day. Using fasting and prayer to get what you need from God and to draw closer to him. Because when we are closer to him, we have everything we need for our mind, body, spirit, and emotions.

Day 18

Description: There is a window when the time is right to attain that specific goal and a favorable moment. Every day that you fast and pray it brings you closer to that favorable time of an opportunity. What we need is the perspective and wisdom to take advantage of those opportunities that God sends our way.

Scripture: Strengthening the souls of the disciples, encouraging them to continue in the faith, and *saying,* "Through many tribulations we must enter the kingdom of God." (Acts 14:22 NASB1995)

Challenge: Many of life's opportunities come disguised as trials and tribulations, that is why fasting, and praying are so very important. Through them our vision is shaped, our perspective is heightened, and our faith is strengthened. During our fasting and prayers journey, we are standing strong on the verge of God-sized opportunities that are requiring faith with action. This time of fasting and prayer is a moment to make the most of your life changes. During our fasting and prayer days embrace what God has for you, lean into it, and listen with your heart and mind. Every one of your life's opportunities has an expiration date. Seize your life's opportunities before their shelf life and yours expire.

Day 19

Description: The smallest amount of faith will produce big results, like the faith of a mustard seed to move a mountain. Your results will have the greatest impact on increasing your faith by fasting and praying with greater confidence and boldness for man's impossible to become God's possible.

Scripture: And He said to them, "Because of the littleness of your faith; for truly I say to you, if you have faith the size of a mustard seed, you will say to this mountain, 'Move from here to there,' and it will move; and nothing will be impossible to you. (Matthew 17:20 NASB1995)

Challenge: What obstacles do you need the Lord's power of fasting and prayer to work through you today? What health challenges have you lacked the faith to ask for in prayer?

Day 20

Description: Life is a marathon; we start off strong and then we "Hit the Wall" almost near the end. We have our ups and downs in our financial lives with bills and prosperity, our physical lives with health and illnesses, our spiritual lives with sins and forgiveness, and our emotional lives with fear and faith. But God is always there, from the beginning of time to the end.

Scripture: The people spoke against God and Moses, "Why have you brought us up out of Egypt to die in the wilderness? For there is no food and no water, and we loathe this miserable food." (Numbers 21:5 NASB1995)

Challenge: Do you feel that you are trapped, what do you need God to deliver you from? Is it financial strain, chronic illness, or deep-seated sin? If that is where you are, don't be afraid because God will fight your battles. Have faith and put your trust in him, call him, and stand firm with your times of fasting and prayer.

Then watch to see the blessings he has for you.

Day 21

Description: People are leaning in to listen and hear you worshipping God. You may feel like you are the only person going through your trials and tribulations, but you are never alone because God is always with you. There are people all around you that are listening and watching to see how you respond to the blessing from God that you have received during your fasting and prayer journey.

Scripture: There you will serve gods, the work of man's hands, work, and stone, which neither see, nor hear, nor eat nor smell. (Deuteronomy 4:28. NASB 1995.)

And He sent them (fasting and prayer) out to proclaim the kingdom of God and to perform healing. (Luke 9:2 NASB1995)

Challenge: Don't feel bad that people are watching you. They have seen you eat healthy and bad foods, and they are paying attention to what is happening in your life because of your fasting and prayer journey. Your words of faith and praise through fasting and prayer will not only lift and heal your heart, but they will touch the hearts and lives of others.

The Journey Continues

The bottom line is people are watching you as you continue your fasting and prayer journey. Move forward with hope expecting that God has heard you and that he is working within, though, and around you in response to the positive changes of your mind, body, spirit, and emotions. God is good all the time for his lovingkindness is everlasting and his grace and mercy for all generations who have faith in him to fast and pray because they are his perfect healing therapies.

"It Takes a Village to Raise a Child and It Also Takes a Village to Heal a Body. Through Fasting and Prayer, Thank You God for Our Healing."

More Personal Stories of Fasting

Margie Collins

I could remember listening to Dr. Hugh A. Jenkins on a local radio station in Chicago Illinois. This was in the late 80s. The message was on fasting and how beneficial it was for the body. After hearing his extensive presentation on fasting, I set up a consultation the next week. I was able to get a special diet according to my health condition. Also, before he put me on a fast, he would create a five-day cleansing diet to scratch the surface of my system. Then proceeding to a longer fast which consisted of seven to twenty-one days. It was beneficial and helpful. It was interesting because after being on the fast for three to four days, I would no longer crave those unhealthy meals. For example, fried fish, fried chicken, French fries, cake, cookies, and pies. This was because I was used to eating those meals. But after going on the fast, my eating habits changed. I lost about fifteen pounds during this period and felt healthy. Right now, I am still his client, and whenever you need some assistance with your health, he will get you back on track with cleansing the body and fasting. Dr. Hugh A. Jenkins is passionate about health and wellness and someone you should know.

David Jenkins

It's August 2019 and I'm coming off an early morning flight from Dallas, Texas after visiting my oldest daughter, my grandchildren, my younger brother Dr. Hugh A. Jenkins and his wife Gwen.

My name is David Jenkins and for the past month my left leg has been swollen from the thigh all the way down to my foot. Now I am concerned, and a few hours after getting off the plane I enter the emergency room, and they tell me I have a blood clot.

I am immediately admitted. They decide to keep me in the hospital, and they start testing. My PSA (normally should be between 0 and 4) is now 673, I did not even know that the PSA could go to three digits.

Now comes the barrage of testing and each time, I'm told I cannot eat before a procedure and so quietly in my private room I found myself fasting and in prayer.

My spiritual path is Eckankar and we chant HU (a love song to God).

The chanting or prayer along with the fasting and only drinking water raised my level of awareness and brought clarity to my situation. Because of the multiple procedures, two biopsies, blood tests, body scans, etc., I was given ample opportunity to fast and pray (chant).

My brother, Dr. Hugh Jenkins was my power of attorney for health and so the doctors freely spoke to him, doctor to doctor, and told him their diagnosis. My brother received their diagnosis before I did, and they told him I have stage 4 prostate cancer that has metastasized to a few bones in my body.

In my contemplation I realized, despite the diagnosis, I was not going to die, and I asked God what was the purpose and what did he want me to do? That little voice that we all hear said, 'journal your journey.' With that I adopted my mindset and said I would be here for another twenty-five years in perfect health and whatever that took it would be successful.

Fast forward my youngest daughter came in from LA and to spend the week with me. Putting me on a vegan diet. So, every morning I spent at least forty-five minutes to an hour before I ate anything in meditation and prayer, which reinforced my mindset of living for another twenty-five or thirty years in perfect health.

My brother had me take a liver flush (cleanse), seven mornings a week, which had me fasting four hours per day for three months straight.

Because of this protocol my PSA went back down to four by April of 2020 with only hormone shots every three months and no radiation, chemotherapy, or surgery.

Fasting and prayer are essential, and it works to raise your level of awareness to make the right decisions for your health or for that matter, anything else in your life.

Thanks to my brother, daughter, and family for their wisdom and guidance.

Gwen Jenkins

When I found Dr. Jenkins in 1987, I had been trying to have a baby for about five years. I had tried some things on my own as I was an avid reader and anything about fasting and nutrition for the purpose of getting pregnant, I picked a few ideas and did them. Like a three, five, and seven day fast, folic acid, and prenatal supplements, to increase my chances of conceiving.

At the time I was in my early 30's and had one child, a fourteen-year-old daughter, but I was having trouble conceiving. I attributed my barrenness to the fact that I decided, after my daughter was born, I would not have any more children. As fate would have it, I met a man some years later who wanted to have a child with me. I believe my desire not to get pregnant again had created my current situation, and I regretted having planted this thought in my subconscious mind.

For over a year, I did the fasting and supple-mentation, but nothing was happening. This did not deter me from my objective. Sometimes I could see the baby I longed for in my dreams. And then one Saturday morning I got up to go to the bathroom and when I got back to my bedroom, something wonderful happened. I got back in bed, intending to get a little more sleep, then I heard a man on the radio talking about working with several women who had come to him trying to get pregnant and he had helped them. I got up, got a pen and paper, and took down the number he gave at the end of the show. I called Dr. Jenkins that day and made an appointment for the following Saturday.

Needless to say, the treatment plan he proposed was nothing like anything I could have imagined. He suggested I go on a forty day fast. I was thinking, forty days without any food, who does that? Of course, Jesus did, but I was just a human woman. Then I thought about it and decided I was willing to do whatever was necessary to have a baby. I had seen him, held him in my arms, and knew he was waiting to come into my life, so I agreed to do the fast.

Dr. Jenkins' fasting regimen was intense. When I told my mother about it, she discouraged me from trying it. In fact, everyone I talked about it thought I was crazy for even thinking of doing it. So, I stopped talking to people about it. I picked up the instructions, tea, and supplements the next weekend and psyched myself out to get ready for this adventure.

The first five days was a cleansing diet to eliminate toxins from my colon and make it easier for me to stay on the fast. It included a strong-tasting tea, morning and evening, and raw fruit. During this cleansing diet, I also took encapsulated herbs. Then the fun really started, forty days of lemon water, herbs to target my problem area, and internal cleansing. I was really surprised to learn that I did not think about food after the third day of the fast. I felt unusually energetic, and my head was clear. I could focus. And I lost five dress sizes! Five...

That fast was a turning point for me. I knew that I could make some unconventional choices using natural therapies that were effective, non-invasive, and had no dangerous side effects. This is how I deal with health challenges now, from a holistic point of view. I am grateful to Dr. Jenkins for having the courage to look beyond conventional allopathic medicine to re-discover the ancient practice of fasting, for a world in need of a different approach to healing.

Dr. Jay P. Vanden Heuvel IMD, PhD

The definition of fasting means the total abstinence from all food for a definite period.

I have done fasting over the decades, usually beginning every New Year's Day which is a good place to start. I have done numerous "fasts" from one day to about three days. My previous record was seven days. But a while ago I decided to go for the long run. I made it fourteen days.

Fasting requires experience. I learned to do one-day, then three-day, then seven-day and finally worked my way up to fourteen-day. There are always a few days prep work prior to starting. Then getting out of a fast (breaking a fast), not too quickly, which goes a few days after as well. So, total fast time can go up to twenty days from beginning to end for this 14 day one. I started out with lowering my food intake a couple days prior, to just a piece of fruit and a few veggies before going for it.

It has certainly given me a new outlook and a never-ending healthy way of life.

I feel from my past experiences that fasting is a 'conviction of a constructive force for body, mind, and spirit'. A valuable part of regular yearly life. Through all practical fasting experience, I lost at times about two pounds of weight per day—safely, with practice and guidance.

I felt my breathing became easier, my movements easier, and a huge increase in energy. Every fast I have ever done.

It is worth noting in physiology that 70 percent of our daily energy requirements are just for the purpose of digestion. So, if we interrupt that process safely, we can divert that 70 percent process to detoxification, energy increase, and rebuilding tissues. Fasting makes sense and I wanted to go farther.

The 14-day fast I am referring to (my longest yet) was full of surprises.

The fast began as did all my previous shorter fasts. After about the third day, I had no desire to eat, whatsoever. I felt no weakness. But if I was ever close to it, I would add a tablespoon of organic maple syrup and a drop of capsicum liquid (no solids allowed) to a glass of water. Like past fasts, when doing the mentioned liquid if weak, I felt like I ate an entire Thanksgiving dinner! How interesting it is to feel that.

My goal of a fourteenth day was not weight loss as much as detoxification. I know how powerful fasting is at cleansing the body, mind, and spirit. But the length here was way more than seven days I completed before. The most powerful thing that happened and it blew my mind, was how on the thirteenth day I was still moving my bowels. Which happened everyday regularly up to that point. But I said out loud on day thirteen, "where is all this coming from?" I had not eaten anything solid in thirteen days. How is that possible?

That really sold me on the benefits of experienced fasting and suggested that I might have been full of it all long.

This was just so amazing. No solid food for almost two weeks, yet my bowels were moving every day. I knew the body was dumping waste, but when would I be empty? This waste (solid) must have accumulated in me over my life in prior decades and it just kept coming. I was dumping years of buildup. Again, I had not eaten anything solid in two weeks. Even as a Doctor of Integrated Medicine for twenty-five years, this was beyond my understanding. My body was dumping waste but not from any recent food—old debris—to brighten my path to becoming healthier and feel younger.

Another body function I noticed was how dark my urine was daily in the first week at times. But by week two, it was clear and light. This helped me understand how the tissues had dumped many toxins and I could now consider maybe ending it after a week. But with the continued solids, I kept going.

My sinuses were clear after eight days. Something I had trouble with for years. My skin was clearer. My mind certainly became much clearer. I was even remembering two to three dreams a night. I felt a more powerful connection to God as well. You cannot put a price on that. As successful as any fast can be, this 14-day fast was amazing. The benefits just kept on coming. I felt in perpetual good health. But by day thirteen my body honestly said "enough". Time to get out and break the fast. Always listen to your inner knowing.

The striking part of such an extended fast (or even a short one) is you do not want to watch television. Every other commercial is about food. In fact, you notice how much food is everywhere and is such a constant. Billboards and even casual conversation seem to always center on food. It is so noticeable.

You overhear in conversations comments such as "I'm starving", "when are we going to eat?" "I could eat a horse" etc. I truly wondered if any one even really knows what it is like to starve, when it has only been a few hours since they last ate. Especially here in an affluent nation of food being everywhere. It does not make any sense. It was so noticeable that the masses were so focused on what, where, and when they would eat next. I just sat back and thought *Wow, I don't need any food, no expense, or grocery buying for a while.* What if everyone practiced this art?

Fasting is such an eye opener as to the non-stop emphasis on food that we consume in this world. Of course, there are many outsides of affluent countries that truly do "starve". I am referring to a 'country of plenty' like the States.

The normal body provides itself with a store of nutrition for vital functions in the absence of food. We were wonderfully made to go "without" at times. Learning to fast with experience, shows you how far it could go. The 14-day one was what I wanted to complete and maybe see how long I could go before my body indicated I should end it. I know from experience, that the body will tell you when it is time to end your fast. On day thirteen I felt that way. Time to break and get out. I did it. I am so proud to have done that and to feel so rejuvenated. Yes, once I slowly brought back food, every bite was eaten slowly, powerfully, yummy and a spiritual experience. It taught me to slow down and enjoy every meal and bite going forward. To give thanks and praise for nourishment from our creator. To not take food for granted, but to eat to live and not live to eat.

Fasting became a new way of life. One needs to work up to extended fasts, such as a fourteen day. It took me a couple New Year's starts to get good at one day fasts, then three-day fasts, then seven-day fasts, before I even attempted a fourteen.

Also keep in mind there is a difference between fasting and starving. Fasting is abstaining from food because reserves in your body allow one to do it safely. Starving is the absence of food after any reserves have been exhausted. Consider your body condition to determine how long you might attempt with guidance. It is common sense and hourly water is critical. I drink water every hour in any fast.

Overall, fasting is a discovery of how the human body, mind, and spirit can rejuvenate. Energy is reallocated to elimination and building, versus constant digestion of non-stop meals. As we have read in the bible, Jesus fasted for spiritual enlightenment and answers. He was, in my opinion, a master faster. Fasting is as old as man. Biblical. Give it a try, I am glad I learned how.

My next goal is twenty-one days. I hope I am still not full of it.

About the Author

Dr. Hugh A. Jenkins became both a Naturopathic and a Chiropractic doctor after years of mentoring by Dr. Alvenia M. Fulton, N.D., a pioneer of natural healing and world authority on fasting. During his many years of practice and mentoring others he was able to assist many people through their journey to Health and Wellness.

Beginning in 2007, he wanted to write a book on fasting and prayers but felt that he did not have enough knowledge in his head to write a successful book. Since that time God has taken him through several life challenges of his body, mind, spirit, and emotions to bring him where he is today.

One of his loving characteristics is that he is a Master of Desert Dry Daddy Jokes. He considers himself a sit-down comedian because he would not make it in stand-up.

Follow me on FaceBook
https://www.facebook.com/groups/438376017017081/

Resources

Davis, L.E., Oyer, R., Beckham, J.D., and Tyler, K.L. "Elevated CSF cytokines in the Jarisch-Herxheimer reaction of general paresis." *JAMA Neurol.* 2013 Aug. 70(8): 1060-4.

Gelfand, J.A., Elin, R.J., Berry, F.W. Jr., and Frank, M.M. "Endotoxemia associated with the Jarisch-Herxheimer reaction." *N Engl J Med.* 1976 Jul 22. 295(4): 211-3. https://pubmed.ncbi.nlm.nih.gov/775337/

Hoekenga, M.T. and Farmer, T.W. "JARISCH- HERXHEIMER REACTION IN NEUROSYPHILIS TREATED WITH PENICILLIN." *Arch Intern Med (Chic).* 1948; 82(6): 611–622. https://jamanetwork.com/journals/jamainternalmedicine/article-abstract/553618

Leonard, Jane. "Seven Ways to do Intermittent Fasting." Medical News today April 16, 2020. https://www.medicalnewstoday.com/articles/322293

Meislin, H.W., and Bremer, J.C. "Jarisch-Herxheimer reaction. Case report." *JACEP.* 1976 October. 5(10): 779-81. https://doi.org/10.1016/S0361-1124(76)80309-7

Pasternak, N.I., and Toporovskiĭ, L.M. "[Clinico-pathophysiologic analysis of the pathogenesis of fever in the Jarisch-Herxheimer-Lukashevich syndrome]." *Vestn Dermatol Venerol*. 1986. (4):21-6. Russian. https://pubmed.ncbi.nlm.nih.gov/3521129/

The Lancet. The Jarisch-Herxheimer Reaction. *ScienceDirect*. 1977 Feb 12. 309(8007): 340-1. https://doi.org/10.1016/S0140-6736(77)91140-0

Web MD. "Fasting: What You Should Know." *Nourish by Web MD*. Last modified October 1, 2020. https://www.webmd.com/diet/obesity/ss/slideshow-fasting-overview?ecd=wnl_wmh_111920&ctr=wnl-wmh-111920_nsl-LeadModule_cta&mb=N9f9087Jc4Tysfb2VVrTmOHnVev1imbCILZoi9tO5NQ%3d

For more great books from Peak Press
Visit Books.GracePointPublishing.com

If you enjoyed reading *Fasting and Prayer* and purchased it through an online retailer, please return to the site and write a review to help others find the book.

www.ingramcontent.com/pod-product-compliance
Lightning Source LLC
LaVergne TN
LVHW020932090426
835512LV00020B/3325